weeknight
gluten free

Recipes and text **Kristine Kidd**

Photographs **Kate Sears**

weldon**owen**

A New Approach to Eating

Good food has always been central to my life, and that love led me to a career as food editor at one of the top epicurean magazines in the country. For more than twenty years, I directed the food content for *Bon Appétit* magazine, delivering delicious recipes to the over seven million readers. It was part of my job to taste all of the recipes we printed. But recently, I had to make a big change in the way I approached food.

I had celiac disease as a baby, and the doctors informed my mother that if I ate no gluten for my first three years, I would be cured. My mom told me this story from the time I was old enough to understand, and I trusted the information, despite digestive problems my entire life. Not long ago, my symptoms became a lot worse, with agonizing bloating almost every time I ate, frequent gastrointestinal distress, and aching joints. The two indicators that really got my attention were fatigue and weight loss, despite eating enormous quantities of dark chocolate to boost my energy (I'm not complaining about that part). After considerable investigation, it became clear that the gluten

intolerance had resurfaced and my system was in chaos. I knew immediately that in order to be happy, I had to eat as well as I always had—fresh, simple, farmers' market–inspired food—but it now had to be free of wheat, rye, barley, and other foods that contain the protein called gluten. Because I am interested in everything about food and cooking, this challenge turned into an enthralling and satisfying project. I attended celiac conferences, read books, and, best of all, experimented in the kitchen.

I hope you enjoy this book with more than 100 gluten-free recipes from a year of glorious experimentation. I organized it by craving, with chapters of dishes you feel like eating: poultry, seafood, and meat. I often like to eat vegetarian (with perhaps some pancetta thrown in for flavor), so I've included a robust meatless chapter, too. There are also a handful of dessert recipes that will satisfy a sweet tooth. In the back of the book, I offer tips and tricks for seasonal, weeknight, and gluten-free eating, including a primer on setting up a gluten-free pantry and a list of sources for some of my favorite gluten-free products.

The approach I developed involves cooking pleasing dishes that are naturally gluten-free, rather than creating disappointing versions of recipes that rely on wheat, rye, or barley. I have tried out dozens of gluten-free pastas that are now available and discovered, to my delight, that a lot of them are really good. I have found excellent quinoa, corn, and mixed-grain products to replace semolina pasta and allow me to keep enjoying many of my favorite classic pasta dishes. I've always loved Asian noodle dishes, too, and then I realized that many of them, made from mung beans or rice, are naturally free of gluten.

Light, flavorful, and modern sauces for main dishes have always been a favorite in my house. Since changing my diet, I have expanded my repertory. Inside this book you'll find many of them: a vibrant salsa verde; pesto laced with nuts, herbs, and lemon; bold vinaigrettes and olive sauces; mayonnaise augmented with fresh herbs; corn or tomato relishes; fresh fruit salsas; and quick guacamole.

For dishes that I used to enjoy with wheat-based pastas or crusty bread, I've come up with several starchy, gluten-free staples that are just as satisfying. Creamy Weeknight Polenta (page 115) takes only minutes to prepare in the microwave. It serves as a satisfying base for sautéed mushrooms or braised chicken or shrimp. Polenta Pizza Crust is made from a similar polenta, spread on a sheet pan and baked (page 51). This transforms it into an excellent foundation for tomato and melted cheese toppings. Quinoa, which takes only minutes to cook, makes a nutritious, high-protein side dish for almost any main dish in my house. There are dozens of ways to add flavor and texture to cooked quinoa (page 75). Socca, naturally gluten-free chickpea pancakes (page 26), can be baked until crisp and then garnished with rich burrata cheese and greens; or cooked into a tender base for sautéed summer squash and Gruyère cheese. I also use socca as a dipper or wrapper in a multitude of ways. Potatoes are a mainstay in my house. Yukon gold potatoes, steamed and then smashed with fresh herbs, olive oil, and a little broth (page 165) are great with sautéed steaks and fish fillets. Cornbread, fragrant, tender, and baked in a cast-iron skillet (page 138) grew from my love of artisan breads. My recipe is so easy, it can be put together on a weeknight and is the dish I am perhaps most excited about in this book. I urge you to get into the kitchen and make one right away.

When I want to enclose foods in wrappers, corn tortillas are a reliable staple. Following Mexican tradition, I toast them over a hot flame and wrap them around almost anything: grilled chicken, sautéed tuna, spicy beef, mashed black beans and feta cheese, and leftovers. Tortillas also make a good replacement for Mandarin pancakes to serve with Easy Mu Shu Pork (page 155). Be sure to check on the label that the tortillas are gluten free. Other wrappers that I developed are Herbed Egg Crepes (page 38), which are actually delicate, super-thin omelets—and they are a joy to make. I fill them with ricotta cheese, sautéed mushrooms, prosciutto, arugula, or any other filling that strikes my fancy.

When I crave crisp crusts on fish or chicken, I use gluten-free ingredients rather than wheat flour or wheat-based bread crumbs to coat them. Dusted with cornmeal or gluten-free flour mix, these tender foods work well for quick sautés. For roasting in a hot oven, I rely on almonds, pecans, and tortilla chips as breadings, but you can also experiment with crushed potato chips and gluten-free corn flakes for kid-friendly meals (page 128).

For weeknight desserts, I depend on fresh seasonal fruit, served with cheese or nuts in the shell, topped with sweetened Greek yogurt, or quickly sautéed and spooned over purchased ice cream. On weekends, I'll bake a big batch of meringue cookies (flavored with spices, nuts, or chocolate chips) and store them in a tin to enjoy after a busy day. Other handy desserts to make on the weekend and have ready in the freezer are oatmeal cookies. Recently, I baked a version for my wedding rehearsal dinner and set them out for guests to enjoy. Not one of them guessed they were gluten-free, and I still get requests for the recipe.

The best part about my new gluten-free lifestyle is that I don't feel deprived. I have served these dishes to my gluten-eating pals, and to my husband, Steve. No one ever noticed anything was missing, nor suspected anything had changed at my table. I hope you and your family will enjoy the recipes from this book as much we do.

Almost Meatless

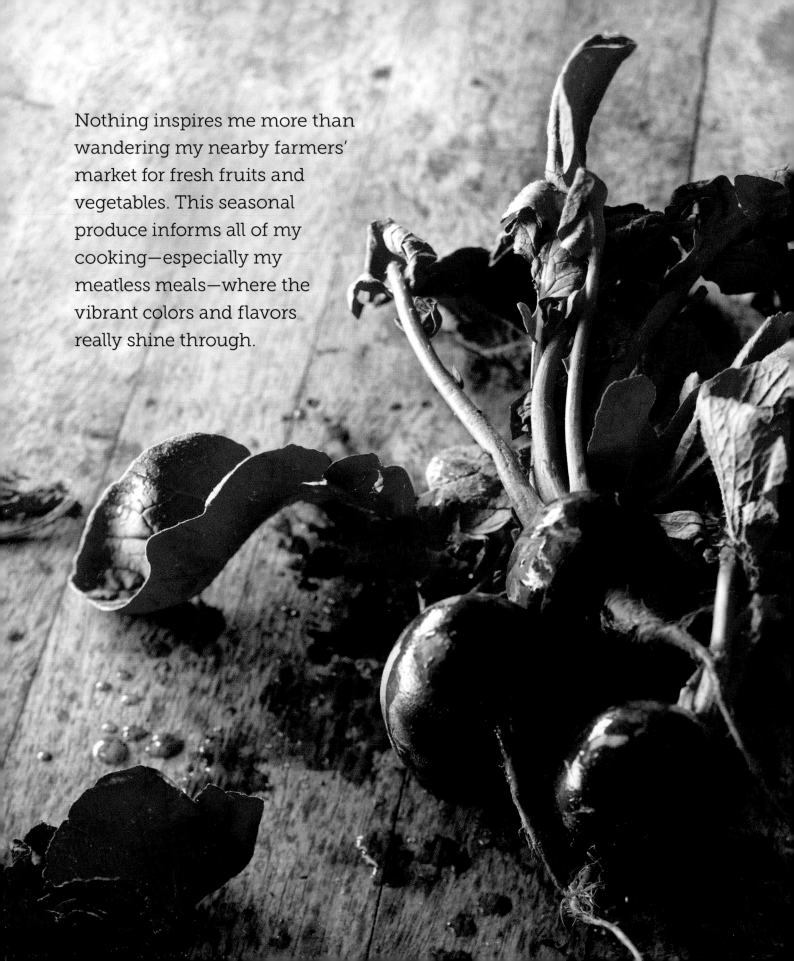

Nothing inspires me more than wandering my nearby farmers' market for fresh fruits and vegetables. This seasonal produce informs all of my cooking—especially my meatless meals—where the vibrant colors and flavors really shine through.

About Meatless Meals

When planning my dinners, I start with fresh produce I find at the farmers' market and let it inspire the other ingredients I add to my meals. While I love to eat seafood, poultry, and meat, I will just as often choose meatless meals, which fit in well with my produce-driven style of cooking and active lifestyle.

Eating vegetarian (almost)

While I am not a vegetarian, I enjoy eating plant-based meals often. But from time to time I like to add a little bit of pancetta (unsmoked, Italian-style bacon) to my recipes. I keep it on hand in my refrigerator, as just a little bit goes a long way to flavor and lend substance to a variety of dishes. Chicken broth also helps lend depth to my otherwise vegetarian recipes, but vegetable broth will also work.

Cooking with the seasons

Quality vegetables are readily available when I use produce that's in season. I also like to plan my dinners based on the weather: lighter dishes in the spring and summer and heartier fare when the weather turns cool. For more on seasonal produce, turn to page 206.

Planting a kitchen garden

Fresh herbs are key to my cooking style. They also help keep vegetarian meals exciting. For my first birthday after we started dating, my now-husband Steve gave me an herb garden. He showed up at my house with terra cotta pots, potting soil, and baby herb plants. We planted them together, and they have become both inspirational and a joy to maintain. Now, I can snip fresh herbs whenever I want them. Even if you don't live in a warm climate, as I do, you can grow herbs in a sunny windowsill.

Storing fresh herbs

If you don't have a cutting garden, buy large bunches of parsley, basil, or cilantro and put them in glasses of water to keep on the kitchen counter for snipping as needed. The herbs will stay fresh for several days. Put other herbs such as thyme, marjoram, or rosemary in a plastic bag, seal the bag with some air enclosed, and store in the refrigerator.

Choosing eggs

Many farmers' markets offer fresh, recently gathered eggs. I like the deep orange color of the yolks and the satisfaction I get from buying from a local farm. An overlooked choice for dinner, eggs are one of the best quick-cooking ingredients for weeknight meals.

Choosing tofu and beans

Protein-rich tofu makes a welcome appearance in my cooking. I love how well it soaks up the flavor of the ingredients cooked with it and its meaty, satisfying texture. Tofu comes in varying densities, but I usually buy firm. It is solid enough to hold its shape while cooking, yet still moist in the center. Sold packed in water or in aseptic packaging, tofu should be drained, rinsed, and then drained again before use. I always choose organic canned beans for my weeknight cooking, as I find their flavor and texture to be superior to regular canned beans.

Crafting a meatless meal

When I'm eating vegetarian, it's essential that the dinner be satisfying enough that I don't feel deprived. I anchor meatless meals with a starchy gluten-free staple such as pasta, quinoa, potatoes, or polenta, and then add hearty ingredients like eggs, mushrooms, and lots of vegetables to keep meals exciting.

Poaching eggs

My favorite way to eat eggs is poached, which I then perch atop a vegetable ragout, polenta, or sautéed greens. Here is my foolproof method for poaching eggs: Fill a large frying pan three-fourths full with salted water and bring to a boil. Add a splash of vinegar. Break an egg into a cup, then slide the egg into the water. Repeat to add the remaining eggs to the pan. Bring the water back to a simmer. Turn off the heat, cover, and let stand until the whites are set, about 2 minutes.

Blanching vegetables

Bring a large pot three-fourths full of water to a boil. Have ready a large bowl of ice water. When the water is boiling, add about 2 teaspoons salt. Add the vegetables to the boiling water. As soon as the vegetables are crisp, barely tender, and brightly colored, after a few seconds, remove them from the water with a skimmer or slotted spoon. Immediately transfer the blanched vegetables to the ice water to stop the cooking and let them stand for a minute or two. Drain and pat the vegetables dry before using in a recipe. For fingerling potatoes, boil them until they are just tender, about 10 minutes. You can skip the ice-water soaking step.

Working with mushrooms

I love using mushrooms in meatless dishes, as their natural umami and texture is as satisfying as meat. Cleaning them is easy: Using a gentle vegetable brush, gently sweep away any dirt from the mushrooms. Use a damp cloth or paper towel to wipe away any stubborn dirt. Avoid rinsing or soaking mushrooms, or they could get soggy. Using a paring knife, trim a thin slice from the base of each mushroom stem. Some varieties, such as shiitake mushrooms, have tough, woody stems, which should be removed before use.

Cooking gluten-free pasta

I find that gluten-free pastas have more of a tendency to stick together than regular wheat pastas. It is important to stir gluten-free pastas—particularly long strand pastas like spaghetti and linguine—as soon as they are added to the cooking water and then stir them frequently throughout the cooking process.

Working with quinoa

This high-protein grain has a natural residue that is very bitter. Rinsing and draining it several times before cooking helps remove this substance, leaving a versatile, mild flavor.

Creamy polenta topped with fried eggs, sautéed greens, and cherry tomatoes cooked until they burst is much better than eggs with toast. This is the dish I used to convince my husband that eggs make a great dinner.

Polenta, Fried Eggs, Greens, and Blistered Tomatoes

Olive oil, 2 tablespoons

Cherry or grape tomatoes, 2 cups (12 oz/375 g)

Red onion, ½ cup (3 oz/90 g) minced

Red pepper flakes

Chard, 1 large bunch, stems removed, chopped

Kosher salt and freshly ground pepper

Large eggs, 4

Creamy Weeknight Polenta (page 115), using thyme

MAKES 2 SERVINGS

Begin the polenta first, and it will be ready to add the herbs and cheese while the eggs are cooking.

1 In a large nonstick frying pan over medium-high heat, warm the oil. Add the tomatoes and cook, stirring occasionally, until blistered, about 4 minutes. Transfer to a bowl. Add the onion and a pinch of pepper flakes to the pan and sauté for 1 minute to soften slightly. Add the chard and sprinkle with salt and black pepper, and stir for 1 minute to coat with oil. Add ¼ cup (2 fl oz/60 ml) water and cook, stirring frequently, until the chard is tender, about 5 minutes. Return the tomatoes to the frying pan and stir for 1 minute to warm. Reduce the heat to medium-low.

2 Using a wooden spoon, make 4 indentations in the mixture. Break an egg into each indentation and sprinkle with salt and black pepper. Cover the pan and cook until the egg whites are set, about 4 minutes.

3 Divide the polenta between 2 warmed plates, spreading it over the center of the plates in a circle. Use a spatula to transfer the eggs and vegetables around them to the plates, arranging atop the polenta. Serve right away.

Creamy and spicy, this intensely flavored dish is based on the pumpkin curry at a local, beachside Thai restaurant. It is naturally gluten-free, the rich texture coming from coconut milk rather than flour.

Thai-Style Tofu and Butternut Squash Curry

For convenience, I use a package of precut butternut squash; if it is unavailable, peel and cut enough squash to measure 2½ cups (about 12 oz/375 g).

I love the nuttiness of brown jasmine rice, and it cooks in the same times as it takes to make the curry.

Use this as a basic recipe, substituting broccoli rabe or kale for the chard, or scallops or cubes of your favorite fish for the tofu.

Vegetable oil, 1 tablespoon

Green onions, 4, white and light green parts sliced separately

Fresh ginger, 3 tablespoons minced

Butternut squash cubes, 1 package (¾–1 lb/375–500 g)

Coconut milk, 1 can (14 oz/430 ml)

Fresh lime juice, 2 tablespoons

Asian fish sauce or gluten-free tamari, 1½ tablespoons

Thai red curry paste, 1 tablespoon

Sugar, 2 teaspoons

Firm tofu, 1 package (14 oz/440 g) drained, cut into ¾-inch pieces

Chard leaves, 2 cups (2 oz/60 g) chopped

Brown jasmine rice (page 214)

Fresh basil, ⅓ cup (½ oz/15 g), sliced

MAKES 4 SERVINGS

1 In a heavy medium pot over medium-low heat, warm the oil. Add the white part of the green onions and the ginger and stir until fragrant, about 2 minutes. Add the squash and stir 1 minute to heat. Add the coconut milk, ¾ cup (6 fl oz/180 ml) water, lime juice, fish sauce, curry paste, and sugar and bring to a simmer. Stir in the tofu. Cover partially and simmer until the squash is just tender, about 20 minutes. Add the chard and cook until wilted, about 2 minutes.

2 Fluff the rice with a fork and divide among 4 warmed bowls. Spoon the curry over. Sprinkle with the green part of the green onions and the basil and serve right away.

Here, mushrooms and pasta are cloaked in a creamy, sage-flecked egg and cheese sauce, with a shower of fresh basil. I like it with a little pancetta, but you can replace it with olive oil for a strictly vegetarian dish.

Mushroom Spaghetti Carbonara

Pancetta, 1½ oz (45 g), chopped, or 1 tablespoon olive oil

Cremini mushrooms, ½ lb (250 g), sliced

Onion, ½, finely diced

Fresh sage, 1 tablespoon minced

Red pepper flakes

Kosher salt and freshly ground pepper

Gluten-free spaghetti, 6 oz (185 g)

Large eggs, 2

Parmesan cheese, ¾ cup (3 oz/85 g) freshly grated

Dry white wine, ¼ cup (2 fl oz/60 ml)

Fresh flat-leaf parsley or basil leaves, ¼ cup (⅓ oz/10 g) torn

MAKES 2 SERVINGS; CAN BE DOUBLED

1 Place a large nonstick frying pan over medium-high heat. Add the pancetta and sauté until beginning to brown, about 3 minutes. Add the mushrooms, onion, sage, and a pinch of pepper flakes. Sprinkle with salt and a generous amount of black pepper. Sauté until the mushrooms are tender, about 8 minutes. Remove the frying pan from the heat.

2 Add the pasta to a large pot of boiling salted water and stir well. Cook, stirring frequently, until al dente, about 8 minutes. Meanwhile, in a small bowl, beat the eggs with a fork and mix in the cheese.

3 Remove ½ cup (4 fl oz/125 ml) of the pasta cooking water and reserve. Drain the pasta. Add the wine to the frying pan with the mushroom mixture and boil until reduced by half, stirring up the browned bits, about 1 minute. Remove the pan from the heat. Add the spaghetti to the frying pan. Gradually whisk ¼ cup (60 ml) of the reserved pasta cooking liquid into the egg mixture. Add the egg mixture to the frying pan and stir until it coats the pasta and is creamy, not wet and runny. If the egg mixture does not become creamy, set the frying pan over very low heat and stir constantly just until it becomes creamy, watching carefully (do not boil).

4 Immediately remove the frying pan from the heat. If needed, mix in enough of the remaining ¼ cup (60 ml) pasta cooking liquid to form a silky texture. Divide between 2 warmed bowls and serve right away.

Gluten-free pasta tends to be stickier than wheat pasta and therefore needs to be stirred thoroughly when first added to the pot of boiling water, and then frequently while cooking.

Dipping ingredients in hummus is so satisfying;
I like to use it as the focal point for an entire meal.
With carrots, fennel, tomatoes, and multigrain tortilla
chips or socca to scoop it, you won't miss pita bread.

Vegetable and Olive Platter with White Bean Hummus

Tahini, a peanut butter-like paste made from ground sesame seeds, is available near the peanut butter in some supermarkets, at natural food stores, and in Middle Eastern stores. Stir it thoroughly before using.

This makes a generous quantity of hummus, so that there is extra to enjoy as a satisfying snack or appetizer another day.

Thin-skinned boiling potatoes, (¾ lb/375 g) cut lengthwise into 1-inch (2.5 cm) wide wedges

Shallot, 1 large, or 2 small garlic cloves, roughly chopped

Cannellini beans, 2 cans (15 oz/ 470 g each), rinsed and drained

Tahini, ½ cup (5 oz/150 g)

Fresh lemon juice, ½ cup (4 fl oz/125 ml)

Extra-virgin olive oil, ¼ cup (2 fl oz/60 ml)

Chile powder, 1½ teaspoons

Fresh dill, ⅓ cup (½ oz/15 g) minced

Kosher salt and freshly ground pepper

Lettuce leaves, such as romaine, little gem, or butter lettuce

Carrots, 1 bunch, peeled and cut into 2-inch (5-cm) pieces

Large fennel bulb, 1, trimmed and sliced

Cherry tomatoes, 1 pint (12 oz/375 g)

Lucques or Kalamata olives, ⅓ cup (4 oz/120 g)

Feta cheese, 3 oz (90 g), cut into ¾-inch (2-cm) chunks

Gluten-free multigrain tortilla chips (I like Food Should Taste Good chips)

MAKES 4 SERVINGS

1 Steam the potato wedges over boiling water until just tender, about 15 minutes. Let cool while preparing the hummus.

2 In a food processor, mince the shallot. Add the cannellini beans, tahini, lemon juice, oil, and chile powder and puree until smooth. Add enough water to thin to the consistency of thick mayonnaise. Mix in the dill. Season to taste with salt and pepper. Transfer to a small bowl.

3 Line a platter with lettuce leaves. Place the bowl of hummus in the center. Arrange the potatoes, carrots, fennel, tomatoes, olives, and cheese in mounds around the hummus. Serve with the tortilla chips.

Inspired by a dish at a favorite restaurant, the creamy cheese topped with a fresh herb sauce is punctuated with crunchy nuts and is so satisfying; I also adore the sauce on grilled seafood, especially salmon, or chicken.

Asparagus with Burrata and Pistachio Salsa Verde

Extra-virgin olive oil, 6 tablespoons (3 fl oz/90 ml)

Fresh basil, ¼ cup (⅓ oz/10 g) finely chopped

Toasted salted pistachio nuts, ¼ cup (1 oz/30 g) finely chopped

Shallot, 2 tablespoons minced

Lemon zest, grated from ½ lemon

Kosher salt and freshly ground pepper

Asparagus, 2 large bunches (about 1½ lb/750 g total), ends trimmed

Burrata cheese, two 4-oz (125-g) balls

MAKES 4 SERVINGS

1 In a small bowl, mix the oil, basil, pistachio nuts, shallot, and lemon zest. Season to taste with salt and pepper.

2 Bring a large frying pan three-fourths full of salted water to a boil. Add the asparagus, cover, and boil until the asparagus is just tender, 4–8 minutes, depending on the thickness of the asparagus. Drain well.

3 Divide the asparagus among 4 warmed plates. Cut each ball of burrata in half and place one half atop the asparagus on each plate, arranging it cut side up. Spoon the salsa verde over the burrata and asparagus and serve right away.

One Sunday morning, I replaced the burrata here with poached eggs for a memorable brunch.

I buy burrata in an 8-ounce (250-g) container, which contains two 4-ounce (125-g) cheese balls.

Popular in Provence, socca is a naturally gluten-free flatbread made from chickpea flour. It can be served on its own as a side dish or accompaniment to a meal. The crisp version (right) can be topped with cheese or salad. The soft version can be topped with your favorite ingredients and eaten like a pizza or wrapped around a filling and enjoyed like a burrito.

Socca

Chickpea (garbanzo bean) flour,
1 cup (4 oz/125 g) for crisp socca or
1¾ cups (7 oz/220 g) for soft socca

Olive oil

Fresh rosemary, 1½ teaspoons minced

Kosher salt and freshly ground pepper

Crisp Socca

In a bowl, combine the 1 cup (4 oz/125 g) flour, 1 cup (8 fl oz/250 ml) room temperature water, 2 tablespoons olive oil, the rosemary, ¾ teaspoon salt, and a generous amount of pepper. Whisk until smooth. Use right away or cover and let stand at room temperature for 30 minutes to 2 hours, or refrigerate overnight.

Arrange the rack in the top part of the oven and preheat to 500°F (260°C). After the oven is fully heated, turn on the broiler, place two 9-inch cake pans in the oven, and heat for 2 minutes. Carefully remove the hot pans from the oven, pour 1 tablespoon oil into each, and swirl to coat the bottoms. Return the pans to the oven until the oil is just smoking, about 2 minutes longer. Carefully remove the pans from the oven and divide the batter between the pans, swirling to cover. Broil until the socca are firm and deeply browned in spots, watching carefully, 7–12 minutes. Serve right away. Makes 2 crisp socca.

Soft Socca

In a bowl, combine 2 cups (16 fl oz/500 ml) water, the 1¾ cups (7 oz/220 g) flour, 1½ tablespoons oil, the rosemary, ¾ teaspoon salt, and a generous amount of pepper. Whisk until smooth. Preheat the oven to 325°F (165° C). Line 2 large baking sheets with parchment paper and brush lightly with oil. Lightly brush a 10-inch (25-cm) nonstick frying pan (with a 7½-inch/19-cm base) with oil and warm over medium-high heat until very hot. Add about one-fourth of the batter and swirl to coat the pan. Cook until air bubbles appear on the top and the bottom is brown, about 2 minutes. Using a silicone spatula, turn the socca over and cook until spotted brown on the bottom, about 1 minute longer. Turn over onto the parchment. Repeat to cook the remaining batter, forming 4 total. Bake for 5 minutes to cook through and serve, or arrange toppings on socca and bake according to the recipe directions. Makes 4 soft socca.

I discovered that socca, a chickpea-based flatbread, makes a wonderful base for creamy burrata cheese. The batter can be whisked together and used right away, but it's even better if it stands for at least 30 minutes.

Crisp Socca with Burrata, Greens, and Olive Dressing

Prepare the dressing and dress the salad while the socca is cooking. It will be ready when you turn out the socca onto plates for serving.

If you can, make the batter the night before or first thing in the morning, and store it in the refrigerator. It will be ready for a quick meal at the end of the day.

Pitted Kalamata olives, ¼ cup (1 oz/30 g)

Extra-virgin olive oil, ⅓ cup (3 fl oz/80 ml)

Red wine vinegar, 2 tablespoons

Freshly ground pepper

Arugula or baby greens, 4 cups (about 4 oz/120 g)

Crisp Socca (page 26)

Burrata cheese, two 4-oz (125-g) balls

MAKES 2 SERVINGS

1 Place the olives in a food processor and process until finely chopped. Add the oil and vinegar and process to blend to make a dressing. Season to taste with pepper (the olives probably contain enough salt already).

2 Place the arugula in a large bowl. Add half of the dressing and toss to coat the leaves well.

3 Turn the browned socca out onto 2 plates. Slice the burrata and spread over the socca. Drizzle with the remaining dressing, and then top with the dressed greens and serve right away.

Tender beans and sweet carrots are infused with enticing spices, and get a dollop of an Indian-inspired yogurt topping. White quinoa is a great substitute for couscous, and it is very high in protein.

Braised Chickpeas and Carrots with Yogurt Topping

Slender carrots, 1 lb (500 g), unpeeled

Olive oil, 4 tablespoons (2 fl oz/60 ml) plus 1½ teaspoons

Large onion, 1, coarsely chopped

Sweet paprika, 2 teaspoons

Ground cumin, 1 teaspoon

Ground cinnamon and ginger, ½ teaspoon *each*

Cayenne pepper, ¼ teaspoon

Chickpeas, 2 cans (15 oz/470 g each), rinsed and drained

Diced tomatoes with juices, 2 cans (14.5 oz/455 g each)

Raisins, 1 cup (6 oz/185 g)

Kosher salt and freshly ground black pepper

Quinoa, 1½ cups (9 oz/92 g)

Plain Greek-style yogurt, ½ cup (4 oz/125 g)

Fresh cilantro leaves and toasted sliced almonds for garnish

MAKES 4 SERVINGS

1 Halve the carrots lengthwise and then quarter them crosswise. In a large nonstick frying pan over medium heat, warm 2 tablespoons of the oil. Add the onion and carrots and sauté until the onion is tender, about 5 minutes. Add the paprika, cumin, cinnamon, ginger, and cayenne and stir for 10 seconds. Add the chickpeas, tomatoes with juices, raisins, and 1 cup (8 fl oz/250 ml) water. Sprinkle with salt and black pepper. Bring to a boil, reduce the heat, cover, and simmer until the carrots are just tender, about 20 minutes.

2 Rinse and drain the quinoa 4 times, and then place in a saucepan. Add 2¼ cups (18 fl oz/560 ml) water and a pinch of salt and bring to a boil. Reduce the heat to low, cover, and simmer until all the water is absorbed, about 15 minutes. Turn off the heat and let stand for at least 5 minutes.

3 In a small bowl, mix the yogurt and 1 tablespoon of the oil. Season to taste with salt and black pepper. Fluff the quinoa with a fork, and then mix in the remaining 1 tablespoon plus 1½ teaspoons oil.

4 Divide the quinoa among warmed plates. Season the chickpea mixture to taste with salt and black pepper and spoon over the quinoa. Spoon the yogurt on top. Sprinkle with cilantro and almonds and serve right away.

For the topping, choose the yogurt you like best—whole milk, two percent, or fat free. No side dish is needed for this complete dish.

At my first dinner in a restaurant with a gluten-free menu, socca pizza was featured, and I was thrilled with this use of the flatbread. The versatile wrapper is pleasantly soft and is easy to put together.

Soft Socca with Summer Squash, Basil, and Gruyère

Vary the topping, as you like: Gouda cheese with sautéed Portobello mushrooms and thinly sliced radicchio; or Gorgonzola cheese and caramelized onions are two I like.

Without a topping, the socca can replace flour tortillas or bread, or wedges can be used to scoop up hummus.

Soft Socca (page 26)

Olive oil, 1½ tablespoons

Red pepper flakes, ½ teaspoon

Yellow squash or zucchini, 1 lb (500 g), sliced

Red onion, 1½ cups (9 oz/280 g) minced

Kosher salt and freshly ground black pepper

Balsamic vinegar, 1 tablespoon

Aged Gruyère or Comté cheese, 2½ cups (about 7 oz/220 g) coarsely grated

Fresh basil, ⅓ cup (½ oz/15 g) chopped

MAKES 4 SERVINGS

1 Preheat the oven to 325°F (165°C). Prepare the socca according to the recipe. Meanwhile, in a large nonstick skillet over medium-high heat, warm the oil. Add the pepper flakes and then the squash and red onion. Sprinkle with salt and black pepper. Sauté until the squash is tender-crisp, about 5 minutes. Add the vinegar and stir until evaporated. Remove from the heat. Taste and adjust the seasoning.

2 Remove the socca from the oven, and sprinkle the cheese over. Divide the squash mixture among the socca. Return to the oven and cook until the cheese melts, about 4 minutes. Transfer 1 socca to each of 4 warmed plates. Sprinkle with basil and serve right away.

There was no way I was going to give up pasta with pesto sauce, bursting with fresh basil, when I went gluten-free, so I sought out great gluten-free pastas. This all-purpose sauce is also good over chicken or fish.

Penne with Walnut Pesto and Peas

Fresh basil leaves, 2 cups (2 oz/60 g) packed

Shallots, 2, or 1 garlic clove, coarsely chopped

Walnuts, ¼ cup (1 oz/30 g)

Lemon zest, 2 teaspoons finely grated

Kosher salt and freshly ground pepper

Extra-virgin olive oil, ¼ cup (2 fl oz/60 ml)

Pecorino romano cheese, ¼ cup (1 oz/30 g) freshly grated, plus more as needed

Gluten-free penne pasta, ½ lb (250 g)

Sugar snap peas, 10 oz (315 g), strings removed

Shelled English peas, 10 oz (315 g), or 1 package (10-oz/310 g) frozen peas

MAKES 4 SERVINGS

1 In a food processor, combine the basil, shallots, walnuts, lemon zest, and ½ teaspoon salt. Process until finely ground. With the machine running, gradually add the oil. Mix in ¼ cup (1 oz/30 g) of the cheese. Season to taste with salt and a generous amount of pepper.

2 Add the pasta to a large pot of boiling salted water and stir well. Cook, stirring occasionally, for about 5 minutes (or 4 minutes less than the cooking time indicated on the package). Add the sugar snaps and peas and cook until the pasta is al dente, stirring occasionally, about 4 minutes longer.

3 Remove ¾ cup (6 fl oz/180 ml) of the pasta cooking water and reserve. Drain the pasta and peas. Put the pesto in a large bowl. Whisk in enough of the reserved cooking water to thin to a sauce. Add the pasta and vegetables and toss to coat. Thin with more cooking liquid and season with salt if needed. Serve right away, passing additional cheese alongside.

Experiment with the many different types and shapes of gluten-free pastas available today to discover your favorite. Look for a list of my favorite gluten-free pastas on page 217.

These quesadillas feature gluten-free corn tortillas instead of the usual wheat flour wrappers. A fresh corn and tomato salsa adds vibrant color and bright flavors. It's an incredibly quick meal to put together.

Black Bean and Feta Quesadillas

Olive oil, 2 tablespoons, plus more as needed

Corn kernels from 1 large ear corn

Kosher salt and freshly ground pepper

Tomato, 1, seeded and chopped

Red onion, 3 tablespoons plus ½ cup (3 oz/90 g) minced

Fresh cilantro, 3 tablespoons minced

Fresh lime juice, 1 tablespoon

Serrano chile, ½ small, seeded and minced

Anise seed, ⅛ teaspoon

Black beans, 1 can (15 oz/470 g) drained, liquid reserved

Gluten-free corn tortillas, 6 (5½–6 inches/14–15 cm in diameter)

Feta cheese, ¾ cup (about 3 oz/90 g) crumbled

Radishes

MAKES 2 SERVINGS; CAN BE DOUBLED

I like to season black beans with a pinch of anise seed, which mimics the subtle taste of wild avocado leaves often used in authentic Mexican cooking.

1 In a large nonstick frying pan over medium-high heat, warm 1 tablespoon of the oil. Add the corn and sprinkle with salt and black pepper. Sauté until just tender-crisp, about 1 minute. Transfer to a bowl. Mix in the tomato, the 3 tablespoons onion, cilantro, lime juice, and chile. Season to taste.

2 In the same frying pan, warm 1 tablespoon oil over medium-high heat. Add the remaining ½ cup (3 oz/90 g) onion and the anise seed and sauté until the onion starts to soften, about 2 minutes. Mix in the drained beans. Simmer, mashing the beans with a spoon to a coarse purée and adding reserved bean liquid if dry. Remove from the heat and season to taste.

3 Heat a griddle or large frying pan over medium-low heat. Brush with olive oil. Add 2 tortillas and cook until softened slightly, about 30 seconds. Turn the tortillas over. Spread 2 tablespoons of the bean mixture over half of each tortilla, leaving a border around the edges. Sprinkle with 2 tablespoons of the cheese. Fold the empty side of the tortillas over the filling and press slightly. Cook until light golden and crisp, about 3 minutes on each side. Transfer to warmed plates. Repeat with the remaining beans and cheese, adding more oil as needed. Divide the quesadillas between warmed plates. Serve right away with the corn salsa for topping and radishes for nibbling.

I loved polenta from the moment I first tasted it in Italy, but never so much as since adopting a gluten-free diet. Here it is a creamy base for mushrooms simmered with shallots, thyme, and wine, and tender poached eggs.

Soft Polenta with Mushroom Ragout and Poached Eggs

Olive oil, 2 tablespoons

Cremini mushrooms, 10 oz (315 g), sliced

Shiitake mushrooms, 3–4 oz (90–125 g) stemmed, thickly sliced

Kosher salt and freshly ground pepper

Shallots, 2, minced

Fresh thyme, 1 tablespoon minced, plus more for garnish

Dry white wine, ⅓ cup (3 fl oz/80 ml)

Tomato paste, 1 teaspoon

Creamy Weeknight Polenta (page 115), using thyme

Poached Eggs (page 16), 2 or 4

MAKES 2 SERVINGS; CAN BE DOUBLED

1 In a large nonstick frying pan over medium-high heat, warm the oil. Add the cremini and shiitake mushrooms and sprinkle with salt and pepper. Sauté until starting to soften, about 3 minutes. Add 3 tablespoons of the shallots and the 1 tablespoon thyme and sauté for 2 minutes. Add the wine and tomato paste and simmer until the liquid becomes syrupy, 1–2 minutes. Adjust the seasoning. Cover and keep warm.

2 Prepare the polenta, adding the remaining shallots to the bowl before cooking. While the polenta cooks, poach the eggs.

3 Divide the polenta between 2 warmed plates, spreading in a circle. Spoon the mushrooms over the polenta. Using a slotted spoon, remove the eggs from the poaching water one at a time, drain off any water, and set atop the mushrooms. Sprinkle the eggs with thyme and pepper and serve right away.

For an even quicker dish, or if I don't have eggs on hand, I replace them with grated Gruyère or crumbled Gorgonzola cheese sprinkled over the mushrooms.

There used to be concerns that blue cheeses contained gluten because the molds used to make them were grown on bread. Today, Gorgonzola and some other blue cheeses have been tested and are gluten free.

Herbed Egg Crepes

As soon as I saw the photo for thin omelets in Yotam Ottolenghi's book, *Plenty,* I was certain they would make a great replacement for crepes. The ones I came up with here are so thin, they resemble crepes, but use no flour, and are wonderfully delicate. You can fill them with almost anything you like; see my favorite fillings at right. To fill the crepes, spread or layer the fillings over half of each crepe. Fold the other half of the crepe over the filling, and then fold them in half again, forming fan shapes. Heat in a 325°F (165°C) oven for about 5 minutes to warm the filling, or serve at room temperature.

Large eggs, 6

Milk, ¼ cup (2 fl oz/60 ml)

Green onions, 4, minced

Mixed fresh herbs, such as flat-leaf parsley, thyme, and tarragon, ½ cup (¾ oz/20 g) minced

Kosher salt and freshly ground pepper

Olive oil, 1 teaspoon, plus more as needed

MAKES 4 CREPES; 2 SERVINGS

Crepes can be filled with a variety of ingredients:

Sautéed sausage, shrimp, or scallops

Sliced prosciutto

Shredded Cheddar, fontina, Gruyère, or Manchego cheese

Crumbled feta or soft fresh goat cheese

Sautéed mushrooms with shredded Gruyère cheese

Sautéed halved cherry tomatoes with crumbled feta or goat cheese

Sautéed dark greens with crumbled feta or goat cheese

Sautéed red bell peppers with shredded Manchego cheese

In a medium bowl, combine the eggs, milk, green onions, mixed herbs, and a pinch each of salt and pepper. Beat with a fork to blend.

Brush a baking sheet with oil. Heat 1 teaspoon oil in a 10-inch (25-cm) nonstick skillet over medium-high heat. Reduce the heat to medium. Add one-fourth of the egg mixture, tipping the pan to cover. Cook until the top of the crepe is set, tipping the pan and spreading the uncooked egg to the edges, 1½ to 2 minutes. Slide the crepe onto the prepared baking sheet. Repeat with the remaining egg mixture, adding more oil to the pan as needed and forming 4 crepes total.

You can play around with different fillings in this irresistible dish: Prosciutto or smoked salmon are good additions to the ricotta, or replace the ricotta with sautéed mushrooms or greens, or shredded Gruyère.

Herbed Egg Crepes with Ricotta and Spring Salad

Whole-milk ricotta cheese,
1 cup (8 oz/250 g)

Green onions, 3, minced

Pecorino romano cheese,
3 tablespoons finely grated

Fresh thyme, 2 teaspoons minced

Olive oil, ¼ cup (2 fl oz/60 ml),
plus more as needed

Kosher salt and freshly ground pepper

Fresh lemon juice, 1 tablespoon

Gluten-free Dijon mustard,
1 teaspoon

Herbed Egg Crepes (page 38)

Baby kale or mixed greens,
3 cups (3 oz/90 g)

Radishes, 6, sliced

**Toasted and salted pistachios
or toasted almonds or pine nuts,**
¼ cup (1 oz/30 g) coarsely chopped

MAKES 2 SERVINGS; CAN BE DOUBLED

I discovered packages of mixed baby kale at the grocery store the last time I made this recipe, and it is worth searching out for the salad. Baby greens are very good too.

1 Preheat the oven to 325°F (165° C). In a medium bowl, mix the ricotta, two-thirds of the green onions, the pecorino cheese, 2 teaspoons thyme, and 1 tablespoon of the oil. Season the filling to taste with salt and pepper. In a small bowl, mix the lemon juice and mustard. Gradually whisk in 3 tablespoons of the oil and the remaining green onions to make a dressing. Season to taste with salt and pepper.

2 Spread one-fourth of the ricotta-herb mixture over half of each egg crepe. Fold each crepe in half over the filling, and then fold in half again, forming fan shapes. Place the crepes in the oven and cook until the filling is warm, about 5 minutes.

3 Meanwhile, combine the kale and radishes in a salad bowl. Add the dressing and toss to coat. Add the nuts and toss. Season to taste with salt and pepper.

4 Arrange 2 filled crepes on each plate. Mound the dressed salad alongside and serve right away.

Inspired by lasagna, grilled eggplant, ripe tomatoes, and creamy cheese seasoned with fresh basil and balsamic vinegar is a fresh and light vegetarian main dish. Wedges of Soft Socca (page 26) are a perfect partner.

Grilled Eggplant, Tomatoes, and Goat Cheese

Extra-virgin olive oil, 6 tablespoons

Fresh basil, ¼ cup (⅓ oz/10 g) minced

Shallots, ¼ cup (1 oz/30 g) minced

Balsamic vinegar, 2 tablespoons

Heirloom tomatoes, 10 oz (315 g), cored and chopped (about 1½ cups/280 g)

Kosher salt and freshly ground pepper

Small, slender Italian eggplants, 4 (about 8 oz/250 g each)

Fresh goat cheese, ¾ cup (about 3 oz/90 g) crumbled

MAKES 4 SERVINGS

Fresh heirloom tomatoes will give the best flavor here. I like Cherokees or Brandywines, but you can choose your favorites.

1 In a small bowl, combine the oil, basil, shallots, and vinegar. In another small bowl, mix the chopped tomatoes and 2 tablespoons of the oil mixture. Season the tomatoes to taste with salt and pepper.

2 Trim the rounded part off 2 opposite long sides of each eggplant. Cut the eggplants lengthwise in half and place on a small oiled baking sheet. Brush both sides with the oil mixture and sprinkle lightly with salt and pepper.

3 Prepare a grill for direct-heat cooking over high heat. Place the eggplant on the grill. Cover and cook until tender, about 8 minutes per side. Return the eggplant to the baking sheet. Divide the cheese among the eggplant halves. Place the baking sheet on the grill, cover, and cook until the cheese begins to soften, about 3 minutes.

4 Using a metal spatula, carefully transfer the topped eggplant to warmed plates. Spoon the tomato mixture over each and serve right away.

In this indulgent dish, pure cream plus aged Gruyère and Parmesan cheeses melt to a creamy consistency and stand in for the traditional flour-thickened sauce. Serve this rich dish with a refreshing romaine salad.

Macaroni and Cheese with Chard and Sage Bread Crumbs

Olive oil, 1½ tablespoons

Large onion, ½, finely chopped

Chard, ½ large bunch, stems trimmed, leaves chopped

Kosher salt and freshly ground pepper

Heavy cream, ½ cup (4 fl oz/125 ml)

Gluten-free elbow or shell pasta, 8 oz (250 g), (I like Ancient Harvest)

Fresh sage, 1 tablespoon minced

Gluten-free bread, 1 slice, ground to crumbs in a food processor (about ½ cup/1 oz/30 g crumbs)

Aged Gruyère cheese, 1 cup (about 3 oz) grated

Parmesan cheese, 2 tablespoons freshly grated

MAKES 4 SERVINGS

1 In a large nonstick skillet over medium heat, warm 1 tablespoon of the oil. Add the onion and sauté until beginning to soften, about 4 minutes. Add the chard and sprinkle with salt and pepper. Sauté until the chard is tender, about 4 minutes. Stir in the cream and remove from the heat.

2 Meanwhile, bring a large pot three-fourths full of salted water to a boil. Add the pasta and stir well. Cook until the pasta is al dente, stirring frequently, about 7 minutes.

3 In a small nonstick skillet over medium heat, warm the remaining ½ tablespoon oil. Add the sage and stir until fragrant, about 30 seconds. Add the bread crumbs and cook until browned and crisp, stirring frequently, about 4 minutes. Season to taste with salt and pepper.

4 Reserve ½ cup (4 fl oz/125 ml) of the pasta cooking water. Drain the pasta. Add the pasta to the skillet with the chard. Add both cheeses and stir over medium heat until the cheeses melt and the pasta is coated, thinning with the pasta cooking liquid as needed. Season to taste with salt and a generous amount of pepper. Divide the pasta among 4 warmed plates. Sprinkle with the bread crumbs and serve right away.

My favorite pasta type for this recipe is made from a mixture of quinoa and corn flour.

This is also good made with aged Cheddar cheese, and the chard can be replaced with any type of cooking greens. If you choose kale, you'll need to sauté it for a few minutes longer than the chard called for here.

Like many people with celiac, I needed to cut down on dairy products at first, but after several months on a gluten-free diet I was able to enjoy cheese again.

This simple, creamy soup has no trace of cream or flour, but is thickened slightly by starch from the beans and is flavored with earthy sage and spicy pepper flakes. I created Skillet Cornbread (page 138) to serve with it.

White Bean, Kale, and Sage Soup

If you can't find low-sodium broth, replace 2 cups (15 fl oz/500 ml) of the broth with 2 cups (15 fl oz/500 ml) water.

Chard is as good as kale in this recipe, and needs only about 3 minutes to wilt into the soup.

Olive oil, 1 tablespoon

Pancetta, 1½ oz (45 g), chopped (optional)

Large onion, 1, finely chopped

Fresh sage, 1 tablespoon minced

Red pepper flakes, ¼ teaspoon

Low-sodium, gluten-free vegetable or chicken broth, 4 cups (32 fl oz/1 l)

White beans, 2 cans (15 oz/470 g each), rinsed and drained

Kale, 1 large bunch, stems removed, coarsely chopped

Kosher salt and freshly ground black pepper

MAKES 4 SERVINGS

1 In a large saucepan over medium heat, warm the oil. Add the pancetta, if using, and sauté for 1 minute. Add the onion, sage, and pepper flakes. Sauté until the onion is translucent, about 8 minutes. Add the broth and the beans. Bring to a boil, reduce the heat to low, and simmer for 20 minutes to develop the flavors, stirring occasionally.

2 Add the chopped kale and simmer until wilted, about 8 minutes. Thin the soup with water if desired. Season to taste with salt and pepper. Ladle into warmed bowls and serve right away.

I created this moderately spiced salad for my cousin's potluck wedding rehearsal dinner, and received many requests for the recipe. It is a good dish to bring to parties, to be certain there is gluten-free food available.

Indian-Style Chickpea Salad

Olive oil, 2 tablespoons

Green onions, 2 bunches, thinly sliced

Fresh ginger, 1 tablespoon minced

Serrano chile, 1, minced with seeds

Fresh cilantro, ½ cup (¾ oz/20 g) chopped

Ground coriander, 1½ teaspoons

Chickpeas, 2 cans (15.5 oz/485 g each) rinsed and drained

Pomegranate molasses, 2 tablespoons

Tomato, 1 large, seeded and chopped

Persian cucumbers, 2 chopped

Plain yogurt, ½ cup (4 oz/125 g)

Ground cumin, ¼ teaspoon

Kosher salt and freshly ground pepper

Romaine heart leaves, warmed gluten-free tortillas, or wedges of Soft Socca (page 26), for serving

MAKES 4 SERVINGS

I like to keep pomegranate molasses, made from pomegranate juice that has been boiled until syrupy, in the cupboard to add an exciting sweet-tart taste to salads, sauces, and stewed dishes.

1 In a large nonstick frying pan over medium-high heat, warm the oil. Add half of the green onions, the ginger, and chile and sauté until tender, about 1 minute. Add ¼ cup (⅓ oz/10 g) of the cilantro and the coriander and stir until fragrant, about 30 seconds. Stir in the chickpeas, pomegranate molasses, and ¼ cup (2 fl oz/60 ml) water. Simmer until the beans are tender and the liquid is absorbed, about 5 minutes. Let cool slightly.

2 Meanwhile, in a large bowl, combine the tomato, cucumber, remaining green onions, and remaining ¼ cup (⅓ oz/10 g) cilantro. In a small bowl, mix together the yogurt and cumin; season to taste with salt.

3 Stir the chickpea mixture into the tomato mixture. Season to taste with salt and black pepper. Divide the salad among 4 plates. Serve with the yogurt sauce, romaine, tortillas, or socca for scooping.

When this uncooked tomato sauce hits the hot pasta, it creates an explosion of summery flavor and fragrance. Use your favorite heirloom varieties, like purple Cherokees, Brandywine, and Sungold cherry tomatoes.

Spaghetti with Heirloom Tomatoes, Olives, and Herbs

Ripe heirloom tomatoes, 1 lb (500 g), cored, halved, seeded, chopped

Heirloom cherry tomatoes, such as Sungold, 1 cup (6 oz/185 g), halved

Mixed fresh herbs, ¼ cup (⅓ oz/10 g) chopped

Pitted Kalamata olives, 3 tablespoons chopped

Extra-virgin olive oil, 2 tablespoons

Shallot, 1½ tablespoons minced

Balsamic vinegar, 2 teaspoons

Kosher salt and freshly ground pepper

Gluten-free spaghetti, 6 oz (185 g)

Feta cheese, ⅓ cup crumbled (about 2 oz/60 g)

MAKES 2 SERVINGS; CAN BE DOUBLED

A young goat cheese is a fresh-tasting alternative to feta. For the herbs, basil, mint, marjoram, thyme, and tarragon are all good choices, in any combination.

Pasta made with corn and quinoa flour works well in this recipe.

I like to make a double recipe and then enjoy leftovers as a cold dish the next day.

1 In a medium bowl, mix the tomatoes, cherry tomatoes, herbs, olives, oil, shallot, and vinegar. Season to taste with salt and pepper.

2 Add the pasta to a large pot of salted water, and stir well. Cook, stirring frequently, until al dente, about 8 minutes. Drain well and place in a warmed pasta bowl. Add the tomato mixture and toss to combine. Gently mix in the cheese. Season to taste and serve right away on 2 warmed plates.

Pizza need not be off-limits if you are living a gluten-free lifestyle. There are many gluten-free pizza crusts available today that are perfect for quick weekday meals, but I enjoy making pizza crusts from polenta, as I like the texture and flavor that it contributes. There's no need to wait for the crust to rise, as with yeast-risen wheat-flour bases, and it is a surprising dish to serve to company. The crust will not be firm enough to pick up, but, enjoyed with a fork, it has the same satisfaction of wheat-flour pizza.

Polenta Pizza Crust

Gluten-free medium-grind cornmeal (I like Bob's Red Mill), 1⅓ cups (7 oz/220 g)

Kosher salt and freshly ground pepper

Olive oil, 1½ tablespoons, plus more as needed

Toppings of your choice (see page 52 for ideas)

In a microwave-safe bowl, mix 4 cups (32 fl oz/1 l) water, the cornmeal, and 1¾ teaspoons salt. Place in the microwave and cook at the high setting for 5 minutes. Stir thoroughly, then return to the microwave and cook at the high setting for 5 more minutes. Stir well. Return to the microwave and cook at the high setting until very thick, about 5 minutes longer. Stir again, and then mix in the 1½ tablespoons olive oil and a generous amount of pepper.

Brush a large pizza pan generously with olive oil. (Do not line the pan with parchment, or the crust will not gain the desired texture.) Spread the cornmeal mixture out on the pan in a circle about ⅓ inch (9 mm) thick and about 12 inches (30 cm) in diameter, building up the edges slightly.

To bake, preheat the oven to 375°F (190°C). Spread tomato sauce, if using, over the cornmeal crust, leaving a border, then layer on the desired toppings. Bake the pizza until it is beginning to brown in spots, about 20 minutes. Let stand for 5 minutes to set up.

Sprinkle the top of the finished pizza with chopped fresh herbs, if desired, then cut into wedges and serve right away.

Gooey cheese melting into baked polenta—crisp on the outside with a creamy interior—is as satisfying as a pizza, but is definitely its own creation. In my house, this one is our new favorite take on the Margherita.

Polenta Pizza with Tomatoes and Fresh Herbs

For a novel approach to pizza, toss baby arugula with olive oil and lemon and mound it atop fontina or mozzarella cheese melted on the finished crust.

More of my favorite toppings for polenta pizza include mozzarella, fontina, feta, or goat cheese; tomato sauce; sautéed mushrooms, bell peppers, onions, or zucchini; gluten-free sausage or pepperoni; pitted olives; halved cherry tomatoes; or chopped fresh herbs.

Fresh mozzarella cheese, ½ lb (250 g) coarsely grated

Polenta Pizza Crust (page 51)

Small cherry tomatoes or grape tomatoes, 1⅓ cups (8 oz/250 g), halved

Shallot, 2 tablespoons minced, or 2 cloves garlic, minced

Olive oil, 1½ tablespoons, plus more as needed

Balsamic vinegar, 1½ teaspoons

Kosher salt and freshly ground pepper

Parmesan cheese, ⅓ cup (1½ oz/45 g) freshly grated

Fresh basil, ¼ cup (⅓ oz/10 g) sliced, or 3 tablespoons chopped fresh marjoram

MAKES 4 SERVINGS

1 Preheat the oven to 375°F (190°C). Sprinkle the mozzarella cheese over the pizza crust on the pizza pan, leaving a border.

2 In a small bowl, mix the tomatoes, shallot, 1½ tablespoons oil, and the vinegar. Season to taste with salt and pepper. Spoon the tomato mixture over the cheese. Sprinkle with the Parmesan cheese.

3 Bake the pizza until it is beginning to brown in spots, about 20 minutes. Let stand for 5 minutes to set up. Sprinkle with the herbs and serve right away with forks and knives for eating.

Here I transform one of my favorite wheat-based dishes into a gluten-free version by substituting high-protein quinoa for bulgur. This recipe gets a flavor boost from feta cheese, fresh mint, and lemon juice.

Quinoa Tabbouleh

Quinoa, 1 cup (6 oz/185 g), preferably multi-color

Kosher salt and freshly ground pepper

Cherry tomatoes, preferably heirloom, 1 lb (500 g), halved

Chickpeas, 1 can (15 oz/470 g), rinsed and well drained

Radishes, 6, chopped

Persian cucumbers, 3, trimmed, quartered lengthwise, cut into ½-inch (12 mm) pieces

Green onions, 4, chopped

Fresh flat-leaf parsley, ¾ cup (1 oz/30 g) chopped

Fresh mint, 3 tablespoons minced

Feta cheese, ½ cup (2½ oz/75 g) crumbled (optional)

Extra-virgin olive oil, ¼ cup (2 fl oz/60 ml)

Fresh lemon juice, ¼ cup (2 fl oz/60 ml)

Romaine hearts

MAKES 4 SERVINGS

1 Place the quinoa in a medium saucepan. Rinse with cold water, drain. Repeat rinsing 3 more times, and then drain the quinoa and return to the pan. Add 1½ cups (12 fl oz/375 ml) water and a pinch of salt and bring to a boil. Reduce the heat to low, cover, and simmer until all the water is absorbed, about 15 minutes. Turn off the heat and let stand at least 5 minutes. Fluff with a fork. Transfer the quinoa to a large shallow bowl and cool to room temperature. (Refrigerate to speed up the cooling).

2 Meanwhile, in a medium bowl, combine the tomatoes, chickpeas, radishes, cucumbers, green onions, parsley, mint, and feta, if using. Add to the cooled quinoa. Add the oil and lemon juice and toss to combine evenly. Season to taste with salt and pepper. Serve with romaine hearts for scooping.

To speed up dinner prep during the week, cook the quinoa the evening before (or save the leftovers from dinner that night).

Instead of the cherry tomatoes, you can use 1 lb (500 g) regular heirloom tomatoes, seeded and chopped.

I like to spoon the salad into a bowl lined with romaine hearts, and then use the salad to pick up bite-sized portions. This is another convenient dish to take to parties.

Golden brown and crisp rosti-style potato pancakes make an ideal base for poached eggs. For best results, use your favorite extra-virgin olive oil for the vibrant green onion and parsley sauce.

Potato Pancakes, Poached Eggs, and Green Onion Sauce

Extra-virgin olive oil, ¼ cup (2 fl oz/60 ml) plus 2 tablespoons, plus more as needed

Fresh flat-leaf parsley, 5 tablespoons (1 oz/30 g) minced

Green onions, 2 tablespoons minced green tops and 3 tablespoons minced white parts

Kosher salt and freshly ground pepper

Russet potatoes, 1 lb (500 g), peeled

Poached Eggs, 4 (page 16)

Plain Greek-style yogurt for serving

MAKES 2 SERVINGS; CAN BE DOUBLED

1 Preheat the oven to 450°F (230°C). Meanwhile, in a small bowl, mix ¼ cup (2 fl oz/60 ml) of the oil, 2 tablespoons of the parsley, the green onion tops, and ¼ teaspoon salt to make a sauce.

2 In a food processor fitted with the coarse grating blade, grate the potatoes. Transfer to a bowl and mix in the remaining 3 tablespoons parsley and the white green onion parts.

3 Working quickly, warm 2 tablespoons oil in a 12-inch (30-cm) nonstick frying pan over medium-high heat. Add about ½ cup (3 oz/90 g) of the potato mixture to the pan and flatten with the back of a spatula into a thin pancake. Repeat, forming 3 more pancakes. Cook until brown and crisp on the first side, about 6 minutes. Sprinkle with salt and pepper, turn over, and cook until brown and crisp on the second side, about 6 minutes. Transfer the potato pancakes to paper towels to drain. Add more oil to the pan and repeat, forming more pancakes. Transfer to paper towels to drain. Transfer the potato pancakes to a baking sheet. Reheat the pancakes in the oven while you poach the eggs.

4 Place 2 potato pancakes on each of 2 warmed plates. Top with the eggs and spoon the green onion sauce over the top. Serve right away with the yogurt and any remaining pancakes on the side.

Seafood

Fish fillets and all kinds of shellfish are mainstays of my cooking repertory, as they cook so quickly and are healthy choices. I am passionate about using only responsibly fished or farmed seafood, and I always choose sustainable species.

About Seafood

Incorporating fish and shellfish dishes into your gluten-free menus is a good way to ensure that you put satisfying, nutritious meals on your table with a minimum of time and effort. Because seafood cooks so quickly, and it is a healthy choice, you'll be able to prepare a memorable meal in just minutes.

Sustainable seafood

Learning about sustainable fish and shellfish can be confusing, because there are so many different names, so many different waters from which they are sourced, and so many ways to catch them. To keep myself current, I rely on the Monterey Bay Aquarium's Seafood Watch program (www.montereybayaquarium.org), which has up-to-date information on the frequently changing topic. From the site, you can print out a pocket guide to take with you to the store or order their mobile app.

Salmon and tuna are some of my all-time favorite types of fish, but they are also some of the most confusing fish available today. I always consult Seafood Watch before I shop and, if I'm at a seafood shop with which I am unfamiliar, I ask a lot of questions. Alaskan salmon and albacore tuna are usually sound choices. Other favorite fish in my house include mahi mahi, Alaskan halibut, black cod, Arctic char, shrimp, scallops, and clams.

Shopping for fish

To find the best-quality fish, start with a reliable fishmonger or the seafood department of a well-stocked food store with frequent turnover. A good fish market will clearly identify its products, where they came from, and how they were harvested and stored.

The staff should be readily able to tell you the origin of a fish and whether it is fresh or previously frozen. They should also willingly skin, fillet, or otherwise prepare the fish to your specifications if you choose not to do it at home. Ask questions: if the answers are vague, consider shopping elsewhere.

Shrimp sizes

Depending on where you live, or where you buy shrimp, labels can be confusing or contradictory. Rather than focusing on size, I like to base my decisions on the number of shrimp in a pound. I've listed both the name and number per pound in my recipes, but here's a helpful reference to help you make decisions when buying shrimp: jumbo (16–20 shrimp per pound) are good for grilling, roasting, simmering, and searing; extra-large (21–25 shrimp per pound) are good for grilling, roasting, and skewers; large (26–30 shrimp per pound) are a good all-purpose size, ideal for salads; medium (31–35 shrimp per pound) work well in stews and fit nicely in a soup spoon.

Be flexible

In many of my recipes, I suggest more than one option for the type of fish or shellfish you can use. If the exact type you are looking for is not available, use one of the alternatives or ask the fishmonger for a suitable substitute.

Working with Seafood

When I crave fish or shellfish during my busy work week, I plan seafood meals for days when I can stop by my favorite fish market on the way home. Fish fillets, shrimp, scallops, or clams all require little extra prep and work wonderfully in a gluten-free lifestyle.

Removing errant bones

I always ask my fishmonger to remove the bones from fillets, but occasionally a few are overlooked. To find stray bones, lay the fillets skin-side down on a work surface and run a fingertip along their length near the center. If you feel the tips of bones sticking up, either pull them out with clean tweezers or needle-nose pliers, or cut out stubborn ones.

Testing fish for doneness

Using the tip of a paring knife, cut into the flesh of the fish and peer inside. Unless you are cooking fish to the rare stage, the interior should be barely opaque, but still very moist. I also like to use a fingertip to gauge doneness; when ready, the flesh should feel springy when lightly pressed. Halibut, in particular, dries out easily, so be careful not to overcook it.

Roasting tips

Pat fish dry with paper towels to facilitate browning and coat with only enough oil to keep the food from sticking to the pan. If the fish has skin, spray the pan with gluten-free cooking spray to prevent sticking.

Grilling tips

I use a gas grill for fish because it is easy to use and convenient for weeknight cooking. It is also easier to control the heat than with a charcoal grill. Brush fish well with oil, and cover the grill for even cooking. If fillets still have the skin, as with salmon, you do not need to turn the fish while cooking; grill the fish skin-side down and the skin will emerge crisp and the flesh moist.

Sautéing tips

Fillets with skin are best cooked in a covered frying pan. Cooked covered, there is no need to turn them and you will end up with crisp skin and moist flesh. If the fillets have been skinned, consider dredging them lightly in gluten-free flour mix or fine cornmeal to protect the delicate flesh from the heat.

Cleaning clams or mussels

Discard any shellfish with cracked or broken shells or shells that don't close to the touch. Place the rest in a bowl of salt water (use ¾ cup/6 oz/185 g salt per 4 quarts/4 l of water) for 10 minutes to purge any sand caught in the shells. If shells still feel gritty after the soaking, scrub them under cold running water with a stiff brush. Remove beards (little fibrous tufts) from mussel shells, if present, by cutting or scraping them away with a paring knife.

So pure and flavorful, Wild Alaskan salmon doesn't need a sauce, but chickpeas simmered in a Moroccan-inspired sauce is a striking accompaniment. The beans absorb the tart, spicy flavorings wonderfully.

Grilled Salmon with Charmoula Chickpeas

Wild salmon fillets, 2 (6 oz/185 g each)

Olive oil, 2 tablespoons, plus more as needed

Kosher salt and freshly ground black pepper

Lemon zest, finely grated from 1 lemon

Ground cumin, 1 teaspoon, plus more as needed

Red onion, ½, chopped

Smoked paprika, 1½ teaspoons

Ground coriander, 1 teaspoon

Cayenne pepper, ⅛ teaspoon

Chickpeas, 1 can (15 oz/470 g), rinsed and drained

Fresh lemon juice, 1 tablespoon

Fresh cilantro, 2 tablespoons minced

MAKES 2 SERVINGS; CAN BE DOUBLED

I like to grill halved slender zucchini or Japanese eggplant along with the fish.

If the weather isn't good for grilling, cook the fish skin side down in a covered skillet.

1 Place the salmon on a plate. Brush with olive oil, then sprinkle with salt, black pepper, lemon zest, and a little cumin.

2 Prepare a grill for direct-heat cooking over high heat. Meanwhile, in a large nonstick frying pan over medium-low heat, warm 2 tablespoons oil. Add the onion and sauté until translucent, about 5 minutes. Add the paprika, the 1 teaspoon cumin, coriander, and cayenne and sauté until fragrant, about 30 seconds. Add the chickpeas and 3 tablespoons water and simmer until the beans are tender, stirring frequently, about 3 minutes. Remove from the heat and mix in the lemon juice. Season to taste with salt and pepper. Cover the pan and keep warm.

3 Place the salmon skin side down on the grill, cover the grill and cook without turning until the salmon is just opaque in the center, about 8 minutes.

4 Divide the salmon and chickpeas between 2 warmed plates. Sprinkle with the cilantro and serve right away.

Similar to aioli, but without the harshness of garlic, this lavish sauce, flavored with lemon and fresh herbs, is a handy gluten-free staple to keep in your refrigerator. It is an elegant accent for grilled albacore and squash.

Grilled Tuna and Vegetables with Fresh Herb Mayonnaise

Not only is this sauce an easy-to-make accompaniment for grilled fish, it makes a creamy dressing for potato salad or coleslaw, a tasty dip for carrot sticks, and keeps for several days in the fridge.

When I don't feel like grilling, I sauté the tuna in a frying pan over medium-high heat.

Fingerling potatoes, 1½ lb (750 g), halved lengthwise

Extra-virgin olive oil, ¼ cup (2 fl oz/60 ml)

Fresh lemon juice, 3 tablespoons

Fresh marjoram, 2 tablespoons minced

Lemon zest, 1 teaspoon grated

Shallot, 1, minced

Gluten-free mayonnaise, ½ cup (4 oz/125 ml)

Albacore tuna steaks, 4 (5–6 oz/155–185 g each)

Assorted summer squash, 1¼ lb (625 g), cut diagonally into ⅓-inch (9-mm) slices

Kosher salt and freshly ground pepper

MAKES 4 SERVINGS

1 In a medium pot of boiling salted water, blanch the potatoes until almost tender, about 10 minutes. Drain.

2 Meanwhile, in a small bowl, mix the oil, lemon juice, 1 tablespoon plus 2 teaspoons of the marjoram, lemon zest, and shallot. In another small bowl, combine 1½ tablespoons of the mixture and the mayonnaise.

3 Place the tuna and squash on a baking sheet. Brush with the olive oil mixture and sprinkle with salt and pepper. In a medium bowl, mix the potatoes and remaining olive oil mixture. Sprinkle with salt and pepper.

4 Prepare a grill for direct-heat cooking over high heat. Add the tuna, squash, and potatoes. Cover and grill just until cooked through, about 5 minutes per side. Transfer the tuna and vegetables to 4 warmed plates. Sprinkle with the remaining 1 teaspoon marjoram. Serve right away with the mayonnaise-herb mixture.

Gluten-free bread, ground into crumbs and mixed with nuts, citrus zest, and a little olive oil, makes a fine topping for fish. Roasted at a high temperature, it emerges crisp and juicy. Serve with roasted broccoli.

Roasted Fish with Lemon-Almond Bread Crumbs

Gluten-free olive oil spray

Fish fillets, such as black cod or wild salmon, 4 (about 6 oz/185 g each)

Olive oil, 1 tablespoon, plus more as needed

Lemon, 1, halved crosswise

Kosher salt and freshly ground pepper

Gluten-free Dijon mustard, about 1 teaspoon

Gluten-free bread, 2 slices

Whole almonds, ½ cup (2½ oz/75 g)

Green onions, 4, finely chopped

Lemon zest, 4 teaspoons finely grated

MAKES 4 SERVINGS

1 Preheat the oven to 450°F (230°C). Spray a rimmed baking sheet with olive oil spray. Place the fish, skin side down, on the pan; brush with olive oil and squeeze the juice from the lemon halves over the fish. Season with salt and pepper, and then spread the mustard lightly over the fillets.

2 Tear the bread into 1-inch pieces. Place in a food processor and grind to fine crumbs. Transfer ½ cup (1 oz/30 g) of the bread crumbs to a small bowl. Grind the almonds coarsely in the processor; add to the bowl with the crumbs. Mix in the green onions, lemon zest, and 1 tablespoon oil. Season to taste with salt and pepper.

3 Just before baking, divide the bread crumb mixture among the fillets, pressing onto the top of each piece. Bake until the fish is just springy to the touch and the bread crumbs start to brown, about 10 minutes, depending on the thickness of the fish. Transfer the fish to plates and serve right away.

When working with lemons, grate the zest first, then cut the fruit in half and squeeze the juice.

This is a great basic recipe to experiment with. I have used walnuts and hazelnuts in place of the almonds, and orange zest instead of lemon. Try it on chicken, too.

Other good fish to try in this recipe include Arctic char, halibut, pacific cod, tilapia, or trout.

Sweet and tender Manila clams, steamed with a little white wine and red pepper flakes and then tossed with pasta strands, is a super-quick and immensely satisfying dinner.

Linguine with Clams, Pancetta, and Tomatoes

Gluten-free linguine or spaghetti, (I like Ancient Harvest), 6–7 oz (200–220 g)

Olive oil, 2 tablespoons

Freshly ground pepper

Pancetta, 1½ oz (45 g) chopped

Shallot, 1 large, thinly sliced

Red pepper flakes

Dry white wine or clam juice, ½ cup (4 fl oz/125 ml)

Manila clams, 2 lb (1 kg)

Fresh flat-leaf parsley, ¼ cup (⅓ oz/10 g) minced

Cherry tomatoes, 1 cup (6 oz/185 g), halved

MAKES 2 SERVINGS; CAN BE DOUBLED

Pastas made with corn and quinoa have a flavor and texture similar to those made with wheat. Linguine is the perfect shape for this zippy sauce. If you can't find linguine, spaghetti works well, too.

1 Add the pasta to a large pot of boiling salted water and stir well. Cook, stirring frequently, until al dente, about 8 minutes. Drain, and then return to the pot. Add 1 tablespoon of oil and a generous amount of pepper and stir to coat. Cover the pot to keep warm.

2 Meanwhile, place a large frying pan over medium heat. Add the remaining 1 tablespoon oil and the pancetta and sauté until beginning to brown, about 2 minutes. Add the shallot and a pinch of pepper flakes and sauté for 1 minute to soften. Add the wine and boil until reduced by half, about 1 minute. Add the clams and half of the parsley. Cover the pan and cook until the clams just open, about 4 minutes. Mix in the tomatoes.

3 Transfer the pasta to a warmed serving bowl. Pour the sauce and clams over the pasta. Sprinkle with the remaining parsley and serve right away.

I like to season fish with olive oil, salt, pepper, and grated lemon zest before cooking, and then serve it with a tempting sauce boasting fresh herbs. This is the place to use a peppery extra-virgin oil.

Grilled Mahi Mahi and Eggplant with Salsa Verde

The sauce takes just a moment to prepare, and is also good with any fish or chicken.

Since olive oil is so prominent here, choose your favorite extra-virgin olive oil with a peppery edge.

Mahi mahi fillets, 4 (5–6 oz/155–185 g each)

Asian eggplants, 1¼–1½ lb (635–750 g), each cut lengthwise into 3 pieces

Extra-virgin olive oil, ¼ cup (2 fl oz/ 60 ml), plus more as needed

Kosher salt and freshly ground pepper

Lemon zest, 1 tablespoon plus 1 teaspoon finely grated

Shallot, 2 tablespoons minced

Fresh flat-leaf parsley, 2 tablespoons minced

Fresh lemon juice, 1 tablespoon

Fresh thyme, 2 teaspoons minced

Red jalapeño, ½, seeded and minced

Brown jasmine or basmati rice for serving (page 214)

MAKES 4 SERVINGS

1 Place the mahi mahi and eggplant slices on a baking sheet. Brush with olive oil on both sides and sprinkle with salt and pepper. Sprinkle the fish with 1 tablespoon of the lemon zest. Let marinate while preparing the sauce.

2 In a small bowl, mix the ¼ cup olive oil, shallot, parsley, lemon juice, thyme, jalapeño, and remaining 1 teaspoon lemon zest. Season to taste with salt and pepper.

3 Prepare a grill for direct-heat cooking over high heat. Add the mahi mahi and eggplant, cover, and grill just until cooked through, about 5 minutes per side. Transfer the mahi mahi and eggplant to 4 warmed plates. Top the fish with the sauce and serve right away.

When a friend came for an impromptu dinner one summer evening, I came up with this Mediterranean-style salad. We scooped it up in lettuce leaves and corn tortillas for a casual supper on my patio.

White Bean, Tuna, Fennel, and Olive Salad

Fennel bulbs, 2, trimmed

Cannellini beans, 2 cans (15 oz/ 470 g each) rinsed and well drained

Albacore tuna in olive oil, 2 cans (5 oz/155 g each) drained, broken into large pieces

Red onion, ½ cup (2½ oz/77 g) finely chopped

Pitted Kalamata olives, ½ cup (2.5 oz/ 77 g), quartered lengthwise

Fresh mint, ¼ cup (⅓ oz/10 g) chopped

Gluten-free Dijon mustard, 2 teaspoons

Fresh lemon juice, 2 tablespoons

Extra-virgin olive oil, ⅓ cup (3 fl oz/80 ml)

Kosher salt and freshly ground pepper

Butter lettuce or romaine lettuce, 1 head

MAKES 4 SERVINGS

1 Cut the fennel bulbs lengthwise into quarters, cut out the core and then slice crosswise. In a large bowl, combine the fennel, beans, tuna, onion, olives, and mint.

2 In a small bowl, place the mustard. Whisk in the lemon juice. Gradually whisk in the oil and a generous amount of pepper. Gently mix into the salad. Season to taste with salt and pepper.

3 Line 4 plates with lettuce leaves, or arrange them on a platter. Mound the salad on top of the lettuce or on another plate and serve.

Look for Wild Planet canned albacore tuna for a sustainable choice. Canned wild Alaskan salmon is a good alternative.

Try leftovers mounded on rice crackers as a snack the next day.

With its mild flavor and hearty texture, quinoa is a gluten-free cook's secret weapon. It can be used as the base for a main-course salad and replaces bulgur wheat or couscous in recipes that call for them. It's also a wonderful side dish for nearly any meal, and with vegetarian dishes to provide extra protein. Use the recipe below as a simple side dish, or use the ideas at right to add flavor, color, and texture.

Basic Quinoa

Quinoa is available in red, white, and multicolor. It cooks in about 20 minutes, making it perfect for weeknight meals.

White, red, or multi-color quinoa, 1 cup (6 oz/185 g)

Kosher salt and freshly ground pepper

Olive oil, 1 tablespoon

Additions of your choice (optional; right)

MAKES 2–4 SERVINGS

Place the quinoa in a medium saucepan. Rinse with cold water, drain. Repeat rinsing 3 more times, and then drain the quinoa and return to the pan. Add 1½ cups (12 fl oz/375 ml) water and a pinch of salt and bring to a boil. Reduce the heat to low, cover, and simmer until all the water is absorbed, about 15 minutes. Turn off the heat and let stand at least 5 minutes before serving.

Fluff the quinoa with a fork, and then mix in the oil and the additions of your choice. Season to taste with salt and pepper.

Quinoa with Fresh Herbs

basil, cilantro, dill, flat-leaf parsley, mint

Change the herb depending on what the quinoa
will be accompanying. You'll need 2–4 tablespoons
chopped fresh herbs.

Quinoa with Vegetables

**baby arugula, radicchio, tomatoes, fennel, persian
cucumbers, red onion, green onions, radishes**

Add different vegetables to contrast or complement
the flavor or texture of the companion dish. You'll need
½–1 cup (4–8 fl oz/125–250 ml) chopped vegetables.

Quinoa with Nuts and Seeds

almonds, hazelnuts, walnuts, pumpkin seeds

If you are serving soft-textured foods, nuts can add
a wonderful texture to contrast with the dish. You'll
need 2–4 tablespoons chopped toasted nuts or seeds.

Quinoa with Other Ingredients

chickpeas, chopped feta, chopped kalamata olives

Almost any ingredient can be mixed into quinoa,
thanks to its neutral flavor. Try the suggestions above,
or experiment with your favorite ingredients. You'll
need ¼–½ cup (2–4 fl oz/60–125 ml).

Quinoa mixed with olive oil and a big handful of fresh herbs makes a refreshing bed for the scallops and zippy salsa made from oranges and avocado. It has become one of my favorite accompaniments to seafood.

Sautéed Scallops and Quinoa with Orange-Avocado Salsa

Oranges, 2, peel and pith removed (page 127)

Large avocado, 1, peeled, pitted, and finely diced

Fresh basil, 3 tablespoons minced

Shallot, 2 tablespoons minced

Red jalapeño, 1½ teaspoons seeded and minced

Kosher salt and freshly ground pepper

Olive oil, 2 tablespoons

Sea scallops, 10–12 oz (315–375 g), patted dry

Basic Quinoa (page 74), using basil as an addition

MAKES 2 SERVINGS

1 Cut the oranges in half, slice them ⅓ inch (9 mm) thick and then cut into ⅓-inch (9-mm) cubes. Place in a bowl. Gently mix in the avocado, basil, shallot and jalapeño. Season to taste with salt and pepper.

2 In a large nonstick frying pan over medium-high heat, warm the oil. Sprinkle the scallops with salt and pepper, add to the pan, and sauté until almost springy to the touch, about 2 minutes on each side.

3 Spread the quinoa on 2 warmed plates. Top with the salsa and then the scallops and serve right away.

The salsa is also good with shrimp or any fish as well as chicken breasts or turkey cutlets.

This recipe makes a generous amount of both the quinoa and salsa because I like to toss them with crumbled feta cheese and pumpkin seeds for a light, but filling, lunch the next day.

To time the dish right, start the quinoa cooking just before making the salsa.

Polenta makes a hearty gluten-free base for this rustic Italian dish. Get the polenta started first, and then simmer the shrimp while it cooks. I like San Marzano tomatoes for their bold flavor and supple texture.

Shrimp in Tomato-Olive-Caper Sauce with Polenta

Look for shrimp from the Gulf of Mexico for a sustainable choice with great taste.

For an equally satisfying variation, replace the shrimp with scallops or cubes of halibut.

Olive oil, 2 teaspoons

Yellow onion, ½, finely chopped

Red pepper flakes

Dry white wine, ⅔ cup (5 fl oz/160 ml)

Tomatoes, 1 can (14.28 oz/440 g), preferably San Marzano

Jumbo shrimp, (16–20 per pound), 10–12 oz (315–390 g), peeled and deveined, tails intact

Kosher salt and freshly ground black pepper

Kalamata olives, ¼ cup (1¼ oz/40 g) pitted, quartered lengthwise

Capers, 1 tablespoon, drained

Fresh thyme, 2 teaspoons minced

Creamy Weeknight Polenta (page 115), using thyme (omit the cheese)

MAKES 2 SERVINGS

1 In a large frying pan over medium heat, warm the oil. Add the onion and a pinch of pepper flakes and sauté until the onion is translucent, about 5 minutes. Add the wine and boil until it is reduced by half, about 4 minutes. Add the tomatoes with their juices. Simmer until the sauce thickens slightly, breaking up the tomatoes with a wooden spoon, about 10 minutes.

2 Sprinkle the shrimp lightly with salt and black pepper. Add to the frying pan, turn to coat with the sauce, cover, and simmer until almost cooked through, about 4 minutes. Mix in the olives, capers, and thyme and simmer until the shrimp are cooked through, about 30 seconds. Taste and adjust the seasoning.

3 Divide the polenta between 2 warmed plates, spreading it out in a circle. Spoon the shrimp and sauce over the top and serve right away.

Smashed potatoes are a great base for moist roasted halibut. The sauce is loaded with briny Kalamata olives, olive oil, and lemon juice and is perfect for the fish as well as the asparagus that is roasted alongside.

Halibut, Asparagus, and Potatoes with Olive Sauce

Pitted Kalamata olives, ⅓ cup (2 oz/60 g) chopped

Extra-virgin olive oil, ¼ cup (2 fl oz/60 ml) plus 2 tablespoons, plus more as needed

Fresh lemon juice, ¼ cup (2 fl oz/60 ml) plus 1 tablespoon

Shallot, 2 tablespoons minced

Fresh thyme, 1 tablespoon plus 1 teaspoon minced

Lemon zest, 1½ teaspoons finely grated

Kosher salt and freshly ground pepper

Asparagus, 2 bunches (about ¾ lb/375 g each), ends trimmed

Halibut fillets, 4 (about 6 oz/185 g each)

Smashed Potatoes with Herbs (page 165)

MAKES 4 SERVINGS

1 Preheat the oven to 450°F (230°C). In a small bowl combine the olives, ¼ cup (2 fl oz/60 ml) of the olive oil, lemon juice, shallot, thyme, and lemon zest. Season to taste with salt and pepper.

2 Place the asparagus on a rimmed baking sheet. Drizzle with 2 tablespoons of the oil and toss to coat. Sprinkle lightly with salt and pepper and toss to coat. Spread in a single layer. Brush a small, rimmed baking sheet with oil, and place the fish on the baking sheet. Transfer 2 tablespoons of the sauce to another small bowl and brush over the fish; sprinkle on both sides with salt and pepper.

3 Roast the asparagus until just tender, 8–10 minutes, depending on their thickness. Roast the fish until almost firm to the touch, 5–8 minutes, depending on the thickness of the fillet.

4 Divide the asparagus among 4 warmed plates. Top with the fish, and spoon the sauce over. Arrange the potatoes alongside and serve right away.

Put the potatoes on to boil as you begin preparations, and they should be ready to smash or crush just before the fish and asparagus finish cooking.

Sautéing the fish skin-side down in a covered skillet is a great technique that yields crisp skin and tender flesh without the need for any flour. A mustard and lemon vinaigrette both seasons the fish and dresses the salad.

Seared Trout with Potatoes and Fresh Herb Salad

Fingerling potatoes, 1½ lb (750 g), halved lengthwise

Extra-virgin olive oil, 2 tablespoons plus ½ cup (4 fl oz/125 ml)

Kosher salt and freshly ground pepper

Gluten-free Dijon mustard, 1 teaspoon

Fresh lemon juice, ¼ cup (2 fl oz/60 ml)

Green onions, 3, 1 minced and 2 thinly sliced

Halibut fillets, 4 (5–6 oz/155–185 g each)

Baby salad greens, 2 cups (2 oz/60 g)

Fresh flat-leaf parsley leaves, 2 cups (2 oz/60 g)

Fresh dill, 1 large bunch, roughly chopped, about ½ cup (½ oz/15 g)

Small fresh basil leaves, ½ cup (½ oz/15 g) packed

MAKES 4 SERVINGS

This recipe is just as good with wild salmon or arctic char.

There will be plenty of vinaigrette left to use another night on a salad or chicken.

1 Preheat the oven to 425°F (220° C). In a large bowl, toss the potatoes with 1 tablespoon of the oil. Sprinkle with salt and pepper and toss to coat. Arrange the potatoes cut side down on a large rimmed baking sheet. Roast until browned on the cut side and tender, about 25 minutes.

2 Meanwhile, in a small bowl, combine the mustard and lemon juice. Gradually whisk in ½ cup (4 fl oz/125 ml) of the oil. Mix in the minced green onion to make a vinaigrette, then season to taste with salt and pepper. Transfer 2 tablespoons of the vinaigrette to a small bowl and brush over the flesh side of the fish. In a salad bowl, combine the greens, parsley, dill, basil leaves, and two-thirds of the sliced green onions.

3 In a 12-inch (30-cm) nonstick frying pan over medium-high heat, warm the remaining 1 tablespoon oil. Add the fish, skin side down. Cover the pan and cook the fish without turning until springy to the touch, about 5 minutes.

4 Dress the salad with vinaigrette to taste and toss well. Divide the salad among 4 warmed plates. Top with the fish, and then drizzle the fish with a little vinaigrette. Arrange the potatoes alongside and serve right away.

Fragrant nuts ground with a hint of lemon and a knob of butter form a crunchy, slightly sweet crust on the fish. Complete the meal with brown jasmine rice (page 214) and a green vegetable.

Mahi Mahi with Pecan Crust

Olive oil

Mahi mahi fillets, 4
(6 oz/185 g each)

Kosher salt and freshly ground pepper

Pecan halves or pieces,
1 cup (4 oz/180 g)

Fresh flat-leaf parsley,
2 tablespoons chopped

Lemon zest, 1 teaspoon finely grated

Butter, at room temperature,
2 tablespoons

MAKES 4 SERVINGS

1 Preheat the oven to 350°F (180°C). Brush oil over a small rimmed baking sheet and place the fish on the sheet. Brush the fish with olive oil and sprinkle with salt and pepper.

2 In a processor, combine the pecans, parsley, and lemon zest. Process to grind finely. Add the butter and blend until the mixture starts to cling together. Spoon the nut mixture onto the top of the fish fillets, pressing to adhere. Roast the fish until it is almost cooked through, about 12 minutes.

3 Position a rack so the fish will be 4 inches from the heat source, and turn on the broiler. Broil the fish until the nuts brown, watching carefully, about 4 minutes. Transfer the fish to 4 warmed plates and serve right away.

This lemony nut crust would be great on salmon or halibut fillets, too.

When buying fish fillets, ask the fishmonger to cut portions into pieces of equal weight and in similar shapes and thickness. This will ensure the fish cooks evenly.

This is my gluten-free take on fish tacos: Spice-coated tuna sautéed until crisp on the outside but slightly pink inside, and a slaw made with sweet shredded broccoli, all topped with a creamy sauce spiked with fresh lime.

Fish Tacos with Broccoli Slaw and Lime Cream Sauce

To toast corn tortillas, set them directly over a gas burner or in a heated dry skillet and cook until a few brown spots appear, about 20 seconds on each side. Keep warm in a tortilla warmer or wrapped in foil.

Prepared broccoli coleslaw, 4 cups (8 oz/250 g), about half of a 16 oz (500 g) bag

Red onion, ¼ cup (1½ oz/45 g) minced

Fresh cilantro, ¼ cup (⅓ oz/10 g) minced

Fresh lime juice, 1 tablespoon plus 2½ teaspoons

Serrano chile, 1, seeded and minced

Kosher salt and freshly ground black pepper

Gluten-free mayonnaise, 6 tablespoons (3 fl oz/90 ml)

Plain Greek-style yogurt, 6 tablespoons (3 oz/90 g)

Lime zest, 1½ teaspoon finely grated

Albacore tuna, 1 lb (500 g), cut into ¾-inch (2 cm) cubes

Ancho chile powder, ¾ teaspoon

Ground cumin, ¼ teaspoon

Ground coriander, ¼ teaspoon

Olive oil, 2 tablespoons

Large avocado, 1, peeled and sliced

Gluten-free corn tortillas, 8–10 (5½–6 inches/14–15 cm in diameter), heated

MAKES 4 SERVINGS

1 In a large bowl, combine the broccoli slaw, onion, cilantro, 1 tablespoon plus 1 teaspoon of the lime juice, and the minced serrano chile. Toss to combine. Season to taste with salt and black pepper. Let the slaw stand while preparing the sauce and fish.

2 In a small bowl, mix together the mayonnaise, yogurt, lime zest, and the remaining 1½ teaspoons lime juice. Mix a pinch of salt into the sauce.

3 In a medium bowl, mix the tuna cubes, chile powder, cumin, and coriander. Sprinkle with salt and black pepper. In a large frying pan over medium-high heat, warm the oil. Add the fish and sauté until brown on the outside but still pink inside, about 2 minutes. Transfer the fish to a warmed bowl.

4 Set out on the table the fish, slaw, sauce, avocado, and tortillas and allow diners to assemble their own tacos.

Instead of dunking crusty, wheat-based bread into the deeply flavored stew, as is tradition, cubes of polenta are added at the last minute. The seafood can be varied by what you find in the market or to your own taste.

Mediterranean Seafood Stew with Polenta Cubes

Gluten-free medium grind cornmeal, 6 tablespoons (2 oz/60 g)

Kosher salt and freshly ground pepper

Olive oil, 2 tablespoons

Yellow onion, 1 large, chopped

Fennel seeds, ½ teaspoon crushed

Red pepper flakes, ¼ teaspoon

Diced tomatoes with juices, 2 cans (14.5 oz/455 g each)

Clam juice, 2 bottles (8 fl oz/250 ml each)

Dry white wine, 1 cup (8 fl oz/250 ml)

Tomato paste, 2 tablespoons

Orange zest, 2 strips (1½-by-½-inches/4-cm-by-12 mm)

Manila clams, 2 lb (1 kg)

Medium shrimp (31–35 per pound), ½ lb (250 g), peeled and deveined

Bay scallops, ½ lb (250 g)

Fresh basil, ⅓ cup (½ oz/15 g) slivered

MAKES 4 SERVINGS

1 In a medium microwave-proof bowl, combine 1½ cups (12 fl oz/375 ml) water and the cornmeal. Microwave at the high setting for 3 minutes. Stir well. Microwave at the high setting for 3 more minutes. Stir well. If the polenta is not thick, microwave at the high setting 1–2 minutes longer. Stir well and season to taste with salt and pepper. Pour out onto a small baking sheet or plate and spread to a rectangle ½ inch (12 mm) thick. Refrigerate until cool and set, at least 15 minutes.

2 Heat the oil in a large pot over medium heat. Add the onion, fennel seeds, and pepper flakes and sauté until the onion is translucent, about 5 minutes. Add the tomatoes, clam juice, wine, tomato paste, and orange zest and bring to a boil. Simmer until slightly thickened and the flavors develop, about 8 minutes. Meanwhile, cut the polenta into ½-inch (12-mm) cubes.

3 Increase the heat to high and add the clams and shrimp to the pot. Cover and boil until the clams start to open, about 4 minutes. Add the scallops and simmer until the shrimp and scallops are cooked through and the clams opened, about 2 minutes longer. Adjust the seasoning. Divide the stew among 4 warmed shallow bowls. Top with the polenta cubes, sprinkle with the basil, and serve right away.

The polenta takes only 5 minutes to cook, and then needs a minimum of 15 minutes to set up in the refrigerator, but even longer is better. If you have time, prepare the polenta the night before.

For a thicker stew, add the polenta cubes to the pot and stir until they dissolve.

Mussels and white fish, such as halibut or cod, are good alternatives to the shrimp, scallops, and clams suggested here, or use only one item.

On summer evenings when I can't stand the idea of turning on any heat source in the kitchen, I like to put together this refreshing salad. I serve crunchy, gluten-free rice crackers alongside.

Asian-Style Shrimp, Tomato, and Cucumber Salad

Shrimp sourced from the waters of the Gulf of Mexico are a good, sustainable choice. Any size is fine for this dish, but I prefer medium to large, rather than jumbo.

Fresh lime juice, 3 tablespoons

Vegetable oil, 3 tablespoons

Asian fish sauce, 1 tablespoon

Serrano chiles, 1½–2, seeded and minced

Shallot, 2 teaspoons minced

Sugar, ½ teaspoon

Kosher salt and freshly ground pepper

Large or medium shrimp (26–35 per pound), 1 lb (500 g) peeled, deveined, and cooked

Persian cucumbers, 6, halved lengthwise, cut crosswise into ½-inch (12 mm) pieces

Heirloom tomatoes, 2 large, cut into ¾–1-inch (2–2.5 cm) pieces

Fresh mint, ⅓ cup (⅓ oz/10 g) small leaves

Fresh basil, ⅓ cup (⅓ oz/10 g) small leaves

Salted peanuts, 3 tablespoons coarsely chopped

Lime wedges for serving

MAKES 4 SERVINGS

1 In a small bowl, mix the lime juice, oil, fish sauce, chiles, shallot, and sugar. Season the dressing to taste with salt and black pepper.

2 In a large bowl, combine the shrimp, cucumbers, and tomatoes. Add the dressing, mint, and basil and toss to combine. Divide the salad among 4 plates. Sprinkle with peanuts. Serve right away with lime wedges to squeeze over the salad.

I developed this favorite recipe in Vermont when a friend brought just-caught brook trout to dinner at my cabin. Earthy tasting cremini mushrooms are cooked just until they start to soften for a meatier texture.

Crispy Trout with Green Onions and Mushrooms

Gluten-free cornmeal, ¼ cup (2 oz/60 g)

Gluten-free flour mix, ¼ cup (1½ oz/ 45 g), (I like Cup4Cup or Bob's Red Mill)

Lemon, 1, cut in half

Trout fillets, 2 (about 6 oz/185 g each)

Kosher salt and freshly ground pepper

Olive oil, 4 tablespoons (2 fl oz/60 ml)

Mushrooms, preferably cremini, 10 oz (315 g), sliced,

Green onions, 5, cut into 1-inch (2.5-cm) pieces

Fresh flat-leaf parsley, 1 tablespoon chopped

MAKES 2 SERVINGS; CAN BE DOUBLED

Cornmeal makes a crunchy, gluten-free alternative to a wheat flour coating. I can never decide whether I prefer the results when I use all cornmeal for a crisper crust, or half cornmeal half gluten-free flour mix, which absorbs the sauce better.

If doubling the recipe, cook the fish in 2 frying pans and the mushrooms in 2 batches, to prevent steaming and keep the coating crisp.

1 On a plate, mix the cornmeal and flour. Squeeze one lemon half over the fish and then sprinkle with salt and pepper.

2 In a large nonstick frying pan over medium-high heat, warm 2 tablespoons of the oil. Add the mushrooms and sprinkle with salt and pepper. Sauté until starting to soften, about 3 minutes. Add the green onions and sauté until the mushrooms are tender-firm, about 2 minutes longer. Transfer to a bowl and cover to keep warm.

3 In another large nonstick frying pan over medium-high heat, warm 2 tablespoons oil. Dip the fish in the flour mixture, coating on both sides. Add to the frying pan, skin side down. Sauté until light brown and the flesh is just springy to the touch, 2–3 minutes per side.

4 Transfer the fish to 2 warmed plates. Squeeze the remaining lemon half over the fish. Spoon the mushroom mixture over the fish. Sprinkle with parsley and serve right away.

In this simple recipe, orange sweet potatoes and bright green kale sauté in one skillet, while fish coated with whole grain mustard cooks in another. I purchase pink-fleshed, delicately flavored char whenever I find it.

Arctic Char with Kale, Sweet Potatoes, and Olives

Olive oil, 3 tablespoons, plus more as needed

Red onion, ½ large, sliced

Red pepper flakes, ¼ teaspoon

Orange-fleshed sweet potato, 1 (about 10 oz/315 g) peeled, quartered lengthwise, and then cut crosswise into ¼-inch (6-mm) thick slices

Kale, 1 bunch, rinsed, stemmed, leaves thinly sliced crosswise, with the water still clinging to them

Kosher salt and freshly ground black pepper

Fresh lemon juice, 2 tablespoons

Arctic char or wild salmon fillets, 4 (about 6 oz/185 g) each)

Gluten-free whole-grain Dijon mustard, about 4 teaspoons

Kalamata olives, ¼ cup (1½ oz/40 g) pitted, cut lengthwise into quarters (optional)

MAKES 4 SERVINGS

Whole-grain mustard does not refer to a gluten-containing grain, but to naturally gluten-free mustard seeds. Still, be certain to read the mustard label to be sure it contains no gluten.

1 In a 12-inch (30-cm) nonstick frying pan over medium-high heat, warm 2 tablespoons of the oil. Add the onion and pepper flakes and sauté for 3 minutes to soften slightly. Add the sweet potato and stir for 1 minute to coat with the oil. Add the kale and stir to coat. Sprinkle lightly with salt and black pepper, and the lemon juice. Cover, reduce the heat to low, and cook, stirring occasionally, until the sweet potatoes are just tender and the kale wilts, about 12 minutes.

2 Meanwhile, brush the flesh of the fish with olive oil, and season with salt and black pepper. Spread the mustard over the top of each fillet. In another large nonstick frying pan over medium-high heat, warm the remaining 1 tablespoon oil. Add the fish skin side down. Cover and cook, without turning, until the fish is just springy to the touch and opaque in the center, about 6 minutes.

3 If using the olives, stir them into the vegetables, and then season them to taste. Divide the vegetables among 4 warmed plates. Place one fish fillet alongside the vegetables on each plate and serve right away.

This Asian-inspired topping for pasta comes together so quickly, it can be prepared while the spaghetti cooks, but remember to stir the gluten-free pasta frequently to prevent it from sticking to itself.

Spaghetti with Shrimp, Asparagus, and Ginger

Gluten-free spaghetti, 6 oz (185 g)

Vegetable oil, 1 tablespoon

Fresh ginger, 3 tablespoons minced

Slender asparagus, 1 large bunch (about 12 oz/375 g), ends trimmed, cut into 1½-inch (4-cm) lengths

Jumbo shrimp, (16–20 per pound), 10 oz (315 g), peeled and deveined

Kosher salt and freshly ground pepper

Asian sesame oil, 2 tablespoons

Green onions, 5, white and light green part thinly sliced

Asian chile paste, such as sambal oelek or Sriracha, 1 teaspoon

Fresh cilantro, ⅓ cup (½ oz/15 g) chopped

MAKES 2 SERVINGS; CAN BE DOUBLED

1 Add the spaghetti to a large pot of boiling salted water and stir well. Cook, stirring frequently, until the pasta is al dente, about 8 minutes.

2 Meanwhile, in a large nonstick frying pan over medium-high heat, warm the vegetable oil. Add the ginger and then the asparagus and cook for 1 minute. Add the shrimp, sprinkle with salt and black pepper, and sauté until the shrimp are just cooked through and the asparagus are crisp-tender, about 6 minutes.

3 Remove ½ cup (4 fl oz/125 ml) of the pasta cooking water and reserve. Drain the pasta, and then add to the frying pan. Add the sesame oil, green onions, and chili paste and stir to coat; add pasta liquid as needed to moisten. Season to taste with salt and pepper. Divide the pasta between 2 warmed plates. Sprinkle with the cilantro and serve right away.

Jumbo shrimp from the Gulf of Mexico are especially tasty and have great texture, but large shrimp can be used too; just add them to the frying pan after cooking the asparagus for 3 minutes.

I make lots of variations on this easy and satisfying dish, replacing the asparagus with zucchini strips or sugar snap peas, and substituting scallops or halibut pieces for the shrimp.

Roasting the green beans deepens their natural flavor and renders them pleasantly crunchy; it is also convenient because they cook along with the fish. Pesto is a terrific gluten-free sauce and is so versatile.

Arctic Char and Green Beans with Arugula-Lemon Pesto

Choose sweet, fresh green beans for this preparation. Older, rubbery ones will not improve when roasted.

Salmon makes an excellent substitute for char.

The pesto is also good on pasta, chicken, and potato salad too. Or swirl into butternut squash or potato soup for a decorative flourish.

Gluten-free nonstick olive oil spray

Arctic char or wild salmon fillets, 4 (about 6 oz/185 g each)

Extra-virgin olive oil, 2 tablespoons, plus more as needed

Minced fresh thyme, 2½ teaspoons

Kosher salt and freshly ground pepper

Green beans, 1 lb (500 g) trimmed

Arugula-Lemon Pesto (page 214)

MAKES 4 SERVINGS

1 Preheat the oven to 450°F (230° C). Spray a small rimmed baking sheet with olive oil spray. Place the fish skin side down on the baking sheet. Brush the fish with olive oil and sprinkle each fillet with ½ teaspoon thyme. Season lightly with salt and pepper.

2 Place the beans in a large bowl. Add the 2 tablespoons oil and sprinkle with salt and pepper. Arrange in a single layer on a larger rimmed baking sheet. Place the beans in the oven and roast until tender-crisp, about 12 minutes. After 4 minutes, place the fish in the oven and roast until just cooked through, about 8 minutes.

3 Divide the beans among 4 warmed plates. Place a fillet on each plate and top with the pesto. Sprinkle the remaining 2 teaspoons thyme over the top and serve right away.

I developed this dish to show off two of my favorite summer ingredients—nectarines and Alaskan salmon. It's so simple to make, and using high-quality ingredients means little embellishment is needed.

Grilled Salmon and Red Onions with Nectarine Salsa

Wild salmon fillets, 4 (6 oz/185 g each)

Olive oil

Kosher salt and freshly ground pepper

Lime zest, finely grated from 1 large lime

Fresh cilantro, 1½ tablespoons plus ¼ cup (⅓ oz/10 g) minced

Red onions, 2, cut crosswise into slices ½–¾ inch (12 mm–2 cm) thick

Nectarines, 1¼ lb (20 oz/625 g), chopped

Red onion, ¼ cup (1½ oz/45 g) minced

Red jalapeño, 1 small, seeded and minced

Fresh lime juice, 1 tablespoon

MAKES 4 SERVINGS

1 Place the salmon skin side down on a baking sheet. Brush with olive oil and sprinkle with salt, black pepper, lime zest, and 1½ tablespoons of the cilantro. Place the onions on the baking sheet. Brush on both sides with oil, and sprinkle with salt and black pepper.

2 In a small bowl, combine the nectarines, remaining ¼ cup (⅓ oz/10 g) cilantro, minced onion, jalapeño, and lime juice. Season to taste with salt and pepper.

3 Prepare a grill for direct-heat cooking over high heat. Place the salmon, skin side down, and the onions on the grill. Cover and cook the salmon without turning until cooked through, about 10 minutes, and the onions until tender and lightly browned, about 5 minutes per side.

4 Divide the salmon and onions among 4 warmed plates. Spoon the salsa over the salmon and serve right away.

Peaches are as good in the salsa as nectarines, and in the fall, try pears instead. Turn the salsa into a fresh chutney by adding a little minced peeled fresh ginger.

At my house, we indulge in grilled wild Alaskan salmon all summer long, enjoying the parade of different varieties: first comes rich king, followed by bright-orange sockeye, and finally delicate silver or coho.

If you'd like a little something extra, serve this with tortillas, rice, or quinoa.

The Mexican flavors in this easy-to-assemble, fresh-tasting dish call for corn chips as an accompaniment. It's a great one to serve during hot weather, as it requires minimal or no cooking.

Shrimp, Avocado, and Peach Salad with Chile and Lime

Make extras of this creamy dressing to use on salads any night of the week.

Fresh lime juice, 1½ tablespoons

Gluten-free mayonnaise, 1 tablespoon

Olive oil, 3 tablespoons

Red onion, 3 tablespoons minced

Red jalapeño, 1, seeded and minced

Kosher salt and freshly ground pepper

Medium shrimp (31–35 per pound), 12–16 oz (390–500 g) peeled, deveined, and cooked, tails intact

Large peaches, 2, sliced

Large avocado, 1, peeled, cut into slices

Fresh cilantro, ⅓ cup (½ oz/15 g) coarsely chopped

Fresh basil, ⅓ cup (½ oz/15 g) coarsely chopped

Romaine hearts, 2, thinly sliced

MAKES 4 SERVINGS

1 In a small bowl, mix the lime juice and mayonnaise. Gradually whisk in the oil. Mix in the onion and jalapeño to make a dressing and season to taste with salt and pepper.

2 In a large shallow bowl, combine the shrimp, peaches, and avocado slices. Add the dressing, cilantro, and basil and gently toss to blend. Add the romaine, toss gently, and serve. Alternatively, divide the romaine among 4 plates, spoon the shrimp-peach mixture over the top, and serve.

Poultry

Chicken and turkey frequently star in
my weeknight meals because they are
lean, cook quickly, and are easy to vary.
I believe organic poultry has the best
flavor and is the most wholesome choice
among what is available.

About Poultry

Versatile and quick-cooking, poultry is a mainstay on my dinner table. Chicken and turkey are also some of the most useful ingredients to have on hand for leftovers because, shredded or sliced, cooked poultry can be easily augmented and used in countless new ways on busy nights.

Choosing poultry

For weeknight cooking, I buy chicken and turkey in pieces that are ready to cook. Among my favorites are boneless, skinless chicken breast halves; chicken breast tenders; and boneless, skinless chicken thighs. Cut from the breast meat and flattened, chicken or turkey cutlets are a wonderful choice for quick sautés.

Bone-in, skin-on chicken pieces are also wonderful raw ingredients for fast meals. The bones and skin both lend a lot of flavor and keep the meat moist during cooking. The skin gains an appealing crispness and golden color when roasted, seared, or grilled. I use assorted bone-in pieces when I am serving a crowd or people with different preferences for white or dark meat. Or, I purchase bone-in breasts, whole legs, or thighs when I am looking for consistent flavor and texture in a dish.

When choosing ground turkey for burgers or chili, I favor dark meat, as it lends more flavor and moisture to a dish than does ground breast meat. To keep things a little leaner, you could also use a mixture of ground dark and white turkey meat.

I favor organic chicken and turkey for its pure flavor. I'm also lucky to live in an area where I have access to locally raised birds that have been treated humanely and have superior taste. I find them at farmers' markets and I enjoy buying them directly from the farmer. If I'm shopping for poultry in a supermarket, I look for "air chilled" on the label, as it is a sign of well-handled meat and a commitment to good taste.

Thinking ahead

Leftover chicken is great to have on hand for quick, gluten-free dinners. I like to roast a whole chicken on the weekend, serve half of it for dinner, and then save the rest for meals during the week. Or, if you are aiming for leftovers, try recipes that call for chicken thighs. The dark meat stays juicy when reheated, while the white meat of chicken breasts can sometimes become dry. Leftover chicken works well in tacos, risotto, chopped salads, and more.

Lightening up

A number of high-quality sausages on the market today are made from chicken and turkey. Used cleverly in risottos, gluten-free pastas, stews, and similar dishes, these poultry sausages can lend surprising depth to dishes without the higher quantity of fat so typical of sausages made from ground pork. As with all sausages, be sure that the poultry sausage is gluten-free; some sausage makers use products that contain gluten as fillers.

Working with poultry

I consider chicken and turkey to be the superheroes of my repertory. When shopping, I often buy extra quantities of boneless chicken breasts or tenders, turkey cutlets, or ground turkey to freeze for later. Thawed overnight, they're ready to incorporate into gluten-free dinners after a long day.

Working with chicken breasts

In a handful of recipes, I call for halving chicken breasts horizontally to help them cook quickly and evenly over high heat. To do this, place the chicken breast on a work surface. Place your non-dominant hand flat on top of the breast to hold it securely, and then use a long, sharp knife to carefully cut the breast in half through the center parallel to the work surface.

Working with chicken legs

For weeknight cooking, I like to separate whole chicken legs into leg and thigh portions. To do this, arrange the chicken leg on a cutting board with the underside facing up. Using a knife, cut through the joint to separate the leg from the thigh.

Testing poultry for doneness

To test boneless cuts of chicken or turkey, use a fingertip to press in the center of the flesh. It should feel firm and spring back right away. To test bone-in cuts, use a paring knife to cut into the flesh near a bone and check to see that the flesh shows no signs of pink and that the juices run clear. For precision, you can also insert an instant-read thermometer into the meatiest part of the cut, away from the bone. When the poultry is done, it should read 165°F (74°C).

Roasting tips

I am an advocate of high-heat roasting, especially for bone-in chicken pieces. Well coated with oil, the skin crisps to a burnished finish and the meat stays moist. Be sure to turn on your kitchen ventilation, as the oven may start to smoke from the high heat.

Grilling tips

When cooking poultry, I like to cover the grill to ensure that it cooks evenly. The air inside the covered grill circulates around the food as it does in an oven to cook it from all sides.

Sautéing tips

Many of the recipes in this chapter—and other chapters— call for sautéing. For best results, select a pan that holds the food comfortably with a little extra space. If the pan is too small, the liquid will collect rather than evaporate and the food will steam rather than sear. If the pan is too large, the oil will tend to smoke and burn.

Thawing frozen cuts

For best results, place frozen poultry in the refrigerator overnight to thaw. It should be ready to cook the next evening.

Salsa verde is a fresh, all-purpose gluten-free sauce we enjoy on poultry, seafood, and pasta. I like to make a double batch to have extra to use another day. If you don't have a grill, the chicken is also delicious sautéed.

Grilled Chicken Breasts with Salsa Verde and White Beans

Salsa Verde (page 215)

Skinless, boneless chicken breast halves, 4 (5–6 oz/155–185 g each)

Kosher salt and freshly ground pepper

White beans, 2 cans (15 oz/470 g each), rinsed and well drained

Cherry tomatoes, 1 pint (12 oz/375 g) halved, or 1 large heirloom tomato, diced

MAKES 4 SERVINGS

1 Prepare a grill for direct-heat cooking over high heat. Set aside ¼ cup (2 fl oz/60 ml) of the Salsa Verde for serving.

2 Place the chicken on a plate. Transfer 2 tablespoons of the salsa verde to a small bowl and brush on both sides of the chicken. Sprinkle lightly with salt and pepper. In a medium bowl, combine the drained beans and tomatoes. Add enough salsa verde to coat. Season to taste with salt and pepper.

3 Place the chicken on the grill, cover, and cook until springy to the touch and cooked through, about 5 minutes on each side. Divide the chicken among 4 warmed plates, and spoon the reserved salsa verde over the top. Spoon the beans alongside and serve right away.

I often serve this white bean and tomato side dish with fish, beef, and lamb dishes. I also wrap it in corn tortillas for easy vegetarian tacos.

The chicken can also be cooked in a covered frying pan over medium heat.

By roasting pieces at a high temperature in place of a whole bird, I have my favorite fall meal in about 30 minutes. Lettuce tossed with mustard vinaigrette makes a refreshing counterpoint to the dish's richness.

Roast Chicken and Vegetables with Fall Spices

Chicken pieces, 2¾–3 lb (1.25 kg–1.5 kg)

Olive oil, 3 tablespoons

Sweet paprika, 2 teaspoons

Ground coriander, 2 teaspoons

Ground cumin, 2 teaspoons

Red pepper flakes, ¾ teaspoon

Lemon zest, grated from 1 large lemon

Kosher salt, 1 teaspoon, plus more as needed

Freshly ground black pepper

Butternut squash pieces, 1 package (14–16 oz/440–500 g)

Fingerling potatoes, 1 lb (500 g), halved lengthwise

MAKES 4 SERVINGS

The vegetables, baked in the same pan as the chicken, are suffused with the fragrant roasting juices and are even better than the bread I used to serve as an accompaniment before I was gluten free.

---

1 Position a rack in the center of the oven, and preheat to 450°F (230°C). Pat the chicken dry, and place in a large bowl; add 2 tablespoons of the oil and turn to coat. In a small bowl, mix the paprika, coriander, cumin, red pepper flakes, and lemon zest. Set aside 1 tablespoon of the spice mixture for the vegetables; add the remainder to the chicken. Add 1 teaspoon salt and a generous amount of black pepper to the chicken and turn to coat. Arrange the chicken, skin side up, on half of a large rimmed baking sheet.

2 Place the squash and potatoes in the same bowl. Add the remaining 1 tablespoon olive oil, season lightly with salt and black pepper, and toss to coat. Add the reserved spice mixture, and toss to coat. Arrange the vegetables on the second half of the baking sheet. Place in the oven and roast until the chicken and vegetables are cooked through, about 25 minutes.

3 Transfer the chicken and vegetables to a warmed platter or 4 warmed plates and serve right away.

Many bakeries are now creating great-tasting gluten-free buns, so you don't need to give up burgers. Or, for an unexpected presentation, place the burgers atop mashed potatoes mixed with a big handful of fresh dill.

Mustard-Dill Turkey Burgers with Mustard-Dill Slaw

Gluten-free mayonnaise, ⅓ cup (3 fl oz/80 ml)

Gluten-free Dijon mustard, 5 tablespoons (2½ oz/75 g)

Fresh dill, 5 tablespoons (½–¾ oz/20 g) minced

Fresh lemon juice, 1 tablespoon plus 1 teaspoon

Kosher salt and freshly ground pepper

Prepared coleslaw mix, 1 bag (8 oz/250 g)

Green onions, 3, minced

Ground turkey, 1¼ lb (20 oz/625 g), preferably dark meat

Olive oil

Toasted gluten-free buns, 4, or **Quick Mashed Potatoes** (page 214), mixed with 2 tablespoons chopped fresh dill

MAKES 4 SERVINGS

1 In a small bowl, combine the mayonnaise, 3 tablespoons of the mustard, 2 tablespoons of the dill, and 1 teaspoon of the lemon juice to make a sauce. Season to taste with pepper. In a large bowl, combine the coleslaw mix, ¼ cup (2 fl oz/60 ml) of the sauce, the remaining 1 tablespoon lemon juice, and one-third of the green onions and toss to coat. Season to taste with salt and pepper.

2 In another large bowl, combine the ground turkey, remaining 2 tablespoons mustard, 3 tablespoons of the dill, the remaining green onions, ¾ teaspoon salt, and a generous amount of pepper. Mix gently. Form the mixture into 4 patties, each about ½ inch thick. Using your thumb, make an indentation in the center of each patty.

3 Heat a large frying pan over medium heat; brush with oil. Add the patties and cook until browned and cooked through in the center, about 5 minutes on each side.

4 Place the bun bottoms on 4 plates or spoon the potatoes in the center of 4 warmed plates. Top each with a patty and a spoonful of sauce. Spoon the coleslaw on top of the patty or alongside the potatoes, place the bun top, if using, over the slaw, and serve right away.

If not everyone in your house eats gluten free, take care when handling condiments. A big risk for people with celiac disease is from people double-dipping in the jars when spreading the sauces on bread or another item that does contain gluten.

Many brands of mayonnaise are gluten free, as are most Dijon mustards. Be sure to read the labels.

Wide pad Thai noodles are made from rice and are naturally free of gluten. They offer the perfect texture for a rich, fragrant sauce and a topping of tender chicken breast, crunchy cabbage, and savory shiitakes.

Sesame-Ginger Noodles with Chicken and Vegetables

To easily shred cabbage into thin strips, first cut the head in quarters lengthwise, cut out the core, and then slice it thinly crosswise.

The stir-fry takes only minutes, but be certain to prepare the ingredients before starting to cook. If using a nonstick pan, use tongs with silicone tips to toss everything together.

Skinless, boneless chicken breast halves, ½ lb (250 g), cut crosswise into slices ¼–⅓ inch (6–9 mm) thick

Fresh ginger, 2 tablespoons minced

Gluten-free tamari, 1 tablespoon plus 2 teaspoons

Asian sesame oil, 3 teaspoons

Rice vinegar, 1 tablespoon plus 1 teaspoon

Kosher salt and freshly ground black pepper

Pad Thai (wide rice) noodles, 8 oz (250 g)

Vegetable oil, 2 tablespoons

Shallot, 1, thinly sliced

Red pepper flakes, ⅛ teaspoon

Napa cabbage, 3 cups (9 oz/180 g) thinly sliced (about ¼ head)

Shiitake mushrooms, 3–4 oz (90–120 g) stemmed and sliced

Gluten-free chicken broth, ¼ cup (2 fl oz/60 ml)

Green onions, 5, thinly sliced

Fresh cilantro, ¼ cup (⅓ oz/10 g) coarsely chopped

MAKES 4 SERVINGS

1 In a bowl, mix the chicken, 1 tablespoon of the ginger, 2 teaspoons of the tamari, 1 teaspoon of the sesame oil, and 1 teaspoon of the rice vinegar. Sprinkle lightly with salt and pepper. Let stand while preparing the noodles.

2 Boil the noodles in a large pot of salted water, stirring frequently, until just tender, about 5 minutes. Drain the noodles, rinse with cold water, and drain again. Place in a bowl, add the remaining 2 teaspoons sesame oil, and toss.

3 In a 12-inch (30-cm) wok or nonstick frying pan over medium-high heat, warm the vegetable oil. Add the remaining 1 tablespoon ginger, the shallot, and red pepper flakes and stir until fragrant, about 30 seconds. Add the chicken and stir until no longer raw on the outside, about 1½ minutes. Add the cabbage and mushrooms and stir until the chicken is cooked through and the cabbage just wilts, 2–3 minutes. Add the noodles, chicken broth, green onions, remaining 1 tablespoon tamari, and 1 tablespoon vinegar. Using tongs, toss until the noodles are heated through and ingredients are well blended, about 1 minute. Season to taste with salt and pepper. Divide among warmed plates, sprinkle with cilantro, and serve right away.

Polenta is a wonderful gluten-free side dish that provides the same rib-sticking satisfaction you get from wheat-based starches, such as pasta or bread. Use it to round out meals of roasted or sautéed meat, poultry, or fish or as a base for a satisfying vegetarian meal topped with either vegetables or poached or fried eggs. You can vary the polenta to your taste with your favorite chopped fresh herbs or grated cheese. If you like, pour the finished polenta into a glass dish, let cool overnight, and then cut into wedges and sauté in olive oil as a crunchy companion to any meal. When serving this with seafood, you may prefer to leave out the cheese.

Creamy Weeknight Polenta

Gluten-free medium-grind cornmeal (I like Bob's Red Mill), ½ cup (2.5 oz/80 g)

Olive oil, 1 tablespoon

Kosher salt and freshly ground pepper

Parmesan or pecorino romano cheese, 2–4 tablespoons freshly grated (optional)

Fresh herbs, 1 tablespoon chopped

MAKES 2–3 SERVINGS

Microwave Method

In a medium microwave-safe bowl, mix 2 cups (16 fl oz/500 ml) water, the cornmeal, oil, ½ teaspoon salt, and a generous amount of pepper. Place in the microwave and cook at the high setting for 5 minutes. Stir thoroughly, then return to the microwave and cook at the high setting for 5 more minutes. Stir well. Mix in the cheese, if using, and herbs, adjust the seasoning, and serve right away.

Stove-top Method

In a heavy saucepan, bring 2½ cups (20 fl oz/625 ml) water, the oil, ½ teaspoon salt, and a generous amount of pepper to a boil over high heat. Gradually whisk in the cornmeal. Bring the mixture back to a boil, stirring frequently. Reduce the heat to low and simmer slowly, stirring frequently, until the polenta is thick, about 18 minutes. Mix in the cheese, if using, and herbs, adjust the seasoning, and serve right away.

Tomato paste is a flavorful gluten-free thickener with the bonus of adding great color to braises and stews. I prefer the products that come in a squeezable tube, because they stay fresh for months.

Braised Chicken and Fennel with Creamy Polenta

Bone-in, skin-on chicken breast halves, 2

Kosher salt and freshly ground pepper

Olive oil, 1 tablespoon

Pancetta, 1½ oz (45 g) chopped

Fennel seeds, 1 teaspoon

Yellow onion, 1, coarsely chopped

Fennel bulb, 1, trimmed, quartered, cored and then sliced, fronds reserved

Bay leaves, 2

Tomato paste, 1 tablespoon

Dry white wine, ½ cup (4 fl oz/125 ml)

Gluten-free chicken broth, ½ cup (4 fl oz/125 ml)

Creamy Weeknight Polenta (page 115), using chopped fennel fronds as the herb

MAKES 2 SERVINGS

1 Using poultry shears, cut the chicken breasts in half crosswise. Pat dry and sprinkle on both sides with salt and pepper. In a large nonstick frying pan over medium-high heat, warm the oil. Add the chicken and cook until brown, about 3 minutes per side. Transfer to a plate.

2 Pour off the fat from the pan and return the pan to medium-high heat. Add the pancetta and fennel seeds and sauté 30 for seconds. Add the onion, sliced fennel bulb, and bay leaves. Sauté until the vegetables begin to brown, about 5 minutes. Stir in the tomato paste. Add the wine and bring to a boil, stirring up the browned bits.

3 Return the chicken to the pan with any juices accumulated on the plate. Add the broth and bring to a boil. Reduce the heat to medium-low, cover, and simmer until the chicken is cooked through, turning after 6 minutes, 12–15 minutes total, depending on the size of the chicken. Taste and adjust the seasoning.

4 Divide the polenta between 2 warmed plates. Top with the chicken and sauce. Sprinkle with minced fennel fronds and serve right away.

Serving creamy polenta as a base for saucy dishes was one of my favorite changes when I was adjusting to a gluten-free diet. My quick version takes just 10 minutes in the microwave, and only needs to be stirred once. It will change the way you think about the grain.

Start the polenta while the chicken is braising in the broth. It will be ready by the time the chicken finishes cooking.

Here, fresh corn and tender chicken breasts are basted with a smoky and spicy mixture and topped with a quick fresh corn relish. Halving the chicken breasts horizontally helps them cook quickly and stay juicy.

Grilled Chipotle Chicken and Corn with Tomato Relish

Ground dried chipotle chile, 1 tablespoon

Ground cumin, 1 tablespoon

Olive oil, 4 tablespoons (2 fl oz/60 ml)

Fresh lime juice, 3 tablespoons

Boneless, skinless chicken breast halves, 1¼–1½ lb (625–750 g)

Fresh corn, 4 ears, husks and silk removed

Kosher salt and freshly ground black pepper

Cherry tomatoes, 1¾ lb (375 g), halved

Green onions, 3 large, halved lengthwise, sliced thinly crosswise

Fresh marjoram, 4 teaspoons plus 1½ tablespoons minced

MAKES 4 SERVINGS

Many brands of canned chipotles in adobo contain gluten, but many pure, ground dried chiles are gluten free and can be found in grocery stores or from online sources.

Try these same flavors on turkey breast cutlets, shrimp, or mahi mahi. Zucchini and other summer squash make a good alternative or addition to the corn.

For indoor cooking, sauté the chicken in a frying pan over medium-high heat and boil the corn. Season the corn after draining.

1 In a small bowl, combine the chipotle chile and cumin. Gradually mix in 3 tablespoons of the olive oil and the lime juice.

2 Using a large knife, carefully cut each chicken breast in half horizontally. Place the chicken and corn on a rimmed baking sheet. Brush on all sides with the chipotle mixture, and then sprinkle lightly with salt and black pepper.

3 In a bowl, combine the tomatoes, green onions, 4 teaspoons of the marjoram, and the remaining 1 tablespoon oil to make a relish. Season to taste with salt and black pepper.

4 Prepare a grill for direct-heat cooking over high heat. Add the corn to the grill rack, cover, and cook until it starts to brown in spots and is almost tender, turning occasionally, about 10 minutes. Add the chicken to the grill rack, cover, and cook until the chicken is springy to the touch and cooked through, 3–4 minutes per side, depending on the thickness of the chicken. Transfer the chicken and corn to a warmed platter. Spoon the relish over the chicken. Sprinkle the corn with the remaining 1½ tablespoons marjoram and serve right away.

Roasting chicken at high heat creates three marvelous things—crisp skin, juicy meat, and drippings too good to throw away—all in about 30 minutes. I deglaze the roasting pan and then toss the juices with pasta.

Roast Chicken with Lemon-Parsley Penne

Chicken pieces, 3 lb (1.5 kg), drumsticks and thighs separated

Olive oil

Kosher salt and freshly ground pepper

Lemon zest, grated from 3 large lemons

Fresh flat-leaf parsley, ½ cup (¾ oz/20 g) minced

Parmesan cheese, ½ cup (2 oz/62 g) freshly grated

Large shallot, 1, minced

Gluten-free penne pasta, 8 oz (250 g) (I like Schar)

Chard, 1 bunch, stems trimmed, leaves chopped

Extra-virgin olive oil, 2 tablespoons

Dry white wine, ½ cup (4 fl oz/125 ml)

MAKES 4 SERVINGS

1 Position a rack in the center of the oven, and preheat to 450°F (230°C). Place the chicken in a metal baking pan. Brush on both sides with olive oil and sprinkle with salt and pepper. Place 2½ tablespoons of the lemon zest in a bowl and set aside; rub the remaining zest into the chicken, then arrange skin side up and roast until cooked through, about 30 minutes. Meanwhile, mix the parsley, Parmesan cheese, and shallot into the reserved lemon zest.

2 Add the pasta to a large pot of boiling salted water and stir well. Cook, stirring frequently, for 2 minutes less than package directions. Add the chard and cook, stirring occasionally, until the pasta is al dente, about 2 minutes. Drain, and then return the pasta and chard to the pot. Add 2 tablespoons extra-virgin olive oil and a generous amount of pepper and stir to coat. Stir in all but 2 tablespoons of the parsley mixture. Cover to keep warm.

3 Transfer the chicken to a warmed platter. Pour off all but a film of fat in the pan, add the wine, and set over medium heat. Bring to a boil, scraping up any browned bits. Pour the mixture into a heavy small saucepan and simmer until reduced to ⅓ cup (3 fl oz/80 ml), about 5 minutes. Pour over the pasta.

4 Divide the chicken among 4 warmed plates and sprinkle with the reserved parsley mixture. Mix any drippings on the chicken platter into the pasta. Adjust the seasonings, divide among the plates, and serve.

When a recipe calls for grated citrus zest, I like to use a Microplane zester. It makes quick work of the 3 lemons called for here.

The flavor, texture, and color of a mixed flour pasta is just right here because it is more similar to semolina wheat pastas than some of the other varieties.

I like the way this richly flavored sauce snuggles into corn and quinoa pasta shells, but you can select any gluten-free pasta from the many options now available. Choose any dark greens you like for this dish.

Pasta with Turkey Sausage and Bitter Greens

Olive oil, 2 tablespoons

Yellow onion, 1 large, chopped

Gluten-free Italian-style turkey sausage, spicy or sweet, 10 oz (315 g), casings removed

Fennel seeds, 1 teaspoon, crushed

Dry white wine, ½ cup (4 fl oz/125 ml)

Gluten-free chicken broth, 1 cup (8 fl oz/250 ml)

Tomato paste, 1 tablespoon

Dark greens, 1 bunch, such as kale or chard, stems removed, chopped

Gluten-free shell pasta, 8 oz (250 g)

Parmesan cheese, ½ cup (2 oz/62 g) freshly grated, plus more for serving

Fresh basil, ¼ cup (¼ oz/8 g) chopped

Kosher salt and freshly ground pepper

MAKES 4 SERVINGS

Be careful to watch gluten-free pastas closely as they are cooking; they quickly progress from hard to al dente to overcooked.

Gluten-free broths in aseptic packages can be resealed. I like to keep one in the refrigerator to add flavor to dishes.

1   In a heavy large frying pan over medium-high heat, warm the oil. Add the onion and sauté until translucent, about 5 minutes. Add the sausage and fennel seeds and cook until the sausage browns, breaking up the sausage with a spoon, about 8 minutes. Add the wine and boil until absorbed, about 2 minutes. Mix in the broth and tomato paste and simmer until the liquid thickens slightly, about 10 minutes.

2   Meanwhile, bring a large pot three-fourths full of salted water to a boil. Add the greens and cook until just tender, 4–6 minutes, depending on the type. Using a slotted spoon, transfer the greens to a bowl. Add the pasta to the pot, stir well, and cook, stirring frequently, until al dente, about 7 minutes. Drain the pasta.

3   Add the greens and pasta to the frying pan and stir to coat with the sauce. Mix in the ½ cup (2 oz/62 g) cheese and the basil. Season to taste with salt and pepper. Divide among 4 warmed plates. Serve right away, passing more cheese alongside.

Fresh herbs and sweet carrots update this old-fashioned skillet dinner. To retain its fragrance, add the thyme just before serving. Skillet Cornbread (page 138), with thyme instead of sage, is a natural accompaniment.

Braised Chicken Thighs with Carrots, Potatoes, and Thyme

Skinless, boneless chicken thighs, 1½ lb (750 g), fat trimmed

Kosher salt and freshly ground pepper

Sweet paprika

Olive oil, 2 tablespoons

Red onion, 1, finely chopped

Red-skinned potatoes, 1 lb (500 g), about 2 inches (5 cm) in diameter, quartered

Carrots, 8, halved lengthwise and then cut into 1½-inch (4-cm) pieces

Gluten-free flour mix, 1 tablespoon plus 1 teaspoon (I like Cup4Cup)

Low-sodium, gluten-free chicken broth, 1⅓ cups (11 fl oz/330 ml)

Dry vermouth or dry white wine, ⅓ cup (3 fl oz/80 ml)

Fresh thyme, 1½ tablespoons minced

MAKES 4 SERVINGS

I was experimenting with Cup4Cup brand gluten-free flour mix as a thickener when I first made this dish, and we loved the silky texture it imparted to the sauce. Try it in your next pan sauce, or experiment with your own favorite flour mix.

1 Season the chicken lightly with salt and pepper and then generously with paprika. In a heavy large frying pan over medium-high heat, warm the oil. Add the chicken and cook until brown, about 2 minutes on each side. Transfer the chicken to a plate. Add the onion to the frying pan and stir. Add the potato quarters and carrots. Sprinkle with salt and pepper and sauté until the vegetables are beginning to brown, about 5 minutes. Add the flour mix and stir to coat. Gradually mix in the broth and vermouth. Bring to a boil, stirring frequently. Return the chicken to the pan and bring to a boil.

2 Cover the pan, reduce the heat to medium-low, and simmer until the chicken and vegetables are cooked through, stirring and turning the chicken over occasionally, about 25 minutes. Mix in the thyme. Taste and adjust the seasoning. Divide the chicken and vegetables among 4 warmed plates and serve right away.

Commercial barbecue sauce often contains gluten. This sweet-spicy version is a delicious alternative, and is so satisfying, gluten-free eaters won't feel left out, and friends will come back for more. Serve with grilled corn.

Grilled Chicken with Quick Barbecue Sauce

For more even cooking, I like to cut large chicken breasts in half crosswise with poultry shears.

The sauce recipe makes a big batch and it keeps for a few days in the fridge, so invite a big group or plan a second grilled dinner later in the week. The sauce is also great on ribs and pork chops.

Olive oil, 1 tablespoon, plus more as needed

Large shallot, 1, minced

Fresh rosemary, 2½ tablespoons minced

Red pepper flakes, ½ teaspoon

Gluten-free ketchup, ¼ cup (2 fl oz/60 ml)

Gluten-free Dijon mustard, ¼ cup (2 oz/60 g)

Light molasses, ¼ cup (2¾ oz/87 g)

Gluten-free chicken broth, ¼ cup (2 fl oz/60 ml)

Smoked paprika, ½ teaspoon

Kosher salt and freshly ground black pepper

Chicken pieces, 3 lb (1.5 kg)

MAKES 4 SERVINGS, WITH EXTRA SAUCE

1 In a medium nonstick skillet over medium heat, warm the 1 tablespoon oil. Add the shallot, 1 tablespoon of the rosemary, and the red pepper flakes and sauté until the shallot is translucent, about 2 minutes. Add the ketchup, mustard, molasses, broth, and smoked paprika. Simmer to blend the flavors, about 10 minutes. Season to taste with salt and black pepper.

2 Meanwhile, brush the chicken with olive oil and then sprinkle with the remaining 1½ tablespoons rosemary, and salt and black pepper to taste.

3 Prepare a grill for direct-heat cooking over high heat. Pour some of the sauce into a bowl for basting. Place the chicken on the grill rack, cover, and cook until browned, about 5 minutes on each side. Brush with the barbecue sauce, cover, and continue to grill until cooked through, basting occasionally with the sauce, about 5 minutes longer on each side. Transfer the chicken to a warmed platter. Serve right away, passing the remaining sauce at the table.

Here is a refreshing, spicy, and tart salad for a night when you want to keep cooking to a minimum. I like to accompany this with gluten-free sweet potato chips, blue corn tortilla chips, or multigrain snack chips.

Chopped Salad with Chicken, Citrus, and Avocado

Fresh lime juice, ⅓ cup (3 fl oz/80 ml)

Olive oil, 9 tablespoons (4.5 fl oz/135 ml)

Red onion, ¾ cup (5 oz/155 g) minced

Large serrano chile, 1, seeded and minced

Ancho chile powder, 1½ teaspoons

Ground cumin, 1 teaspoon

Kosher salt and freshly ground pepper

Skinless, boneless chicken breast halves, 1–1¼ lb (20 oz/625 g)

Oranges, 2

Cherry tomatoes, 1 pint (12 oz/375 g), halved

Fresh cilantro, ½ cup (⅔ oz/20 g) coarsely chopped

Romaine hearts, 4 cups thickly sliced (about 4 oz/120 g)

Large avocado, 1, peeled and cut into bite-sized pieces

MAKES 4 SERVINGS

1 In a small bowl, place the lime juice. Gradually whisk in the olive oil. Mix in the onion, serrano chile, ancho chile powder, and cumin to make a dressing. Season the dressing to taste with salt and black pepper. Transfer 2 tablespoons of the dressing to another small bowl and brush over the chicken. Let the chicken stand while preparing the remaining ingredients.

2 Using a thin, sharp knife, remove the skin and white pith from the oranges. Cut them lengthwise in quarters, then slice crosswise. In a large bowl, combine the oranges, tomatoes, and cilantro.

3 Heat a large nonstick frying pan over medium heat. Add the chicken, cover the pan, and cook until just cooked through, 5–8 minutes on each side, depending on the thickness of the chicken. Transfer the chicken to a cutting board and let cool for 10 minutes.

4 Cut the chicken into bite-sized pieces and add to the bowl with the oranges and tomatoes. Mix in half of the remaining dressing. Add the romaine and the remaining dressing and toss to coat. Season the salad to taste with salt and black pepper. Gently fold in the avocado and serve right away.

To work with oranges and other citrus, cut off a thin slice from the top and bottom of the fruit to expose the flesh. Stand the fruit on the cutting board on a flat end. Following the curve of the fruit, and working from top to bottom, cut away the peel and white pith from the flesh. Continue in this fashion, working your way around the fruit.

If heirloom tomatoes look good in the market, replace the cherry tomatoes with 1 large heirloom tomato, halved, seeded, and chopped.

Crunchy, golden-brown breaded items are always crowd-pleasers, but they often use wheat-based items to create the crust. Since changing the way I eat, I've discovered that a number of gluten-free ingredients can create the same crisp satisfaction in just minutes. Below is a basic formula for creating baked breaded chicken, turkey, or fish at home. Or turn to page 83 for a terrific nut-crusted fish or page 130 for an easy way to bread bone-in chicken pieces.

Gluten-Free Breadings

Gluten-free canola-oil spray

Breading of choice such as almonds, gluten-free cornflakes, gluten-free tortilla chips, pecans, or potato chips

Dried herbs such as thyme, oregano, or marjoram (optional)

Spices such as cayenne, chili powder, or paprika (optional)

Thin cuts of poultry or fish, such as chicken tenders, chicken or turkey cutlets, or medium-thick fish fillets

Olive oil

Kosher salt and freshly ground pepper

Baking Method

Preheat the oven to 450°F (230°C). Spray a rimmed baking sheet with canola oil spray. If necessary, in a food processor, process large items like corn flakes, tortilla chips, potato chips, and nuts until finely ground. If using nuts, take care not to process them too finely, or they will turn into nut butter. Transfer the breading to a glass dish and add a small amount of dried herbs or spices to taste.

Brush the chicken, turkey, or fish with olive oil and season generously with salt and pepper. Add the poultry or fish to the breading mixture and turn to coat all sides, pressing the crumbs into the surface with your fingertips to help them adhere; place on the prepared baking sheet. Spray the tops of the breaded item with additional canola oil spray to encourage browning. Bake until the breading is golden brown and the poultry or fish is cooked through, 10–15 minutes, depending on thickness.

It's easy to create a crisp coating on thin pieces of poultry or fish: dredge them lightly in gluten-free flour mix or cornmeal, shake off the excess, then sauté in butter or oil in a hot pan until cooked through.

Turn to page 91 for my take on cornmeal-crusted trout or page 134 for a wonderful chicken tenders sauté with garden vegetables.

Before using them as a coating, sure to read the labels on packages of chips or cereal to make sure they are gluten free.

Finely ground gluten-free tortilla chips make a crunchy coating, and high-heat roasting produces moist, flavorful meat without the mess of frying. Choose chicken legs, thighs, or breasts, with or without skin, as you prefer.

Oven "Fried" Chicken with Baby Spinach Salad

Olive oil, ¼ cup (2 fl oz/60 ml), plus more as needed

Gluten-free tortilla chips, 1 bag (5½ oz /170 g) (I like Food Should Taste Good Multigrain chips)

Dried marjoram, 1 teaspoon, crumbled

Ground cumin, 1 teaspoon

Cayenne pepper, ¼ teaspoon

Chicken pieces, 3½ lb (1.75 kg)

Kosher salt and freshly ground pepper

Fresh lime juice, 2 tablespoons

Baby spinach, 4–6 oz (125–185 g)

Cherry tomatoes, 1 pint (12 oz/375 g), halved

MAKES 4–6 SERVINGS

This is a great choice for an easy family supper or picnic. For more gluten-free breading ideas, turn to page 128.

1 Preheat the oven to 450°F (230°C). Brush a large rimmed baking sheet with oil. Meanwhile, in a food processor, grind the tortilla chips finely and transfer to a pie plate. Mix in the marjoram, cumin, and cayenne pepper. Brush the chicken on all sides generously with oil, and then sprinkle with salt and pepper. Add the chicken to the crumb mixture, 2 pieces at a time, and turn to coat on all sides, pressing into the crumbs to help them adhere. Arrange the pieces skin side up on the baking sheet.

2 Place in the oven and roast until the crust is brown and the chicken is cooked through, about 35 minutes. Let stand for 5 minutes to crisp.

3 In a small bowl, place the lime juice. Gradually whisk in the ¼ cup olive oil to make a vinaigrette. Season to taste with salt and pepper. In a salad bowl, combine the spinach and tomatoes. Add the vinaigrette and toss to coat. Divide the chicken and salad among plates and serve.

Chicken and vegetables are bathed in a quick Korean-inspired sauce that is also good on fish. Nutty-flavored, slightly sticky short-grain brown rice is a delightful gluten-free accompaniment.

Asian-Flavored Chicken with Shiitakes and Bok Choy

Olive oil, 4 tablespoons (2 fl oz/60 ml)

Shallot, 1, minced

Fresh ginger, 1 tablespoon minced

Serrano chile with seeds, 1½ teaspoons minced

Gluten-free tamari, ⅓ cup (3 fl oz/80 ml)

Brown sugar, ¼ cup (2 oz/60 g) firmly packed

Unseasoned rice vinegar, 3 tablespoons

Asian sesame oil, 1 tablespoon

Skinless, boneless chicken thighs, 1¼–1½ lb

Kosher salt and freshly ground pepper

Baby bok choy, 6, halved lengthwise

Fresh shiitake mushrooms, 8 oz (250 g), stemmed

Green onions, 4, thinly sliced

Cooked short-grain brown rice for serving

MAKES 4 SERVINGS

1 In a heavy small saucepan over medium heat, warm 1 tablespoon of the olive oil. Add the shallot, ginger, and chile and sauté until tender, about 3 minutes. Add the tamari, brown sugar, vinegar, and 3 tablespoons water and simmer until the mixture is reduced to ¾ cup (6 fl oz/180 ml), about 6 minutes. Remove from the heat and stir in the sesame oil. Transfer half of the mixture to another small bowl.

2 In a large bowl, place the chicken. Add 1 tablespoon of the olive oil and salt and pepper to taste and toss to coat. In another large bowl, combine the bok choy and mushrooms. Add the remaining 2 tablespoons olive oil, and salt and pepper to taste, and toss to coat.

3 Prepare a grill for direct-heat cooking over high heat. Place the chicken on the grill rack and brush with sauce from one of the bowls. Place the vegetables on the grill rack. Cover the grill and cook the chicken until cooked through, brushing occasionally with the sauce, about 6 minutes per side. Cook the vegetables until tender-crisp and browned, about 4 minutes per side. Transfer the chicken and vegetables to a warmed platter and sprinkle with the green onions. Serve right away with the rice and remaining sauce.

For a quick snack or hearty breakfast, I like to simmer leftover cooked rice with almond milk, brown sugar, and a cardamom pod until heated through.

Think of this easy recipe as a template, substituting asparagus or zucchini for the peas, and tarragon or dill for the mint. I love to spoon it over brown jasmine rice (page 214) or Basic Quinoa (page 74).

Sautéed Chicken Tenders with Peas and Mint

Chicken tenders are great for weeknights because they cook quickly and need little preparation.

Gluten-free flour mixes are easy to use, form a golden brown coating on the chicken, and thicken the sauce to a silky texture.

Gluten-free flour mix for dredging (I like Cup4Cup)

Chicken tenders, 10 oz (315 g)

Kosher salt and freshly ground pepper

Olive oil, 2 tablespoons

Shelled fresh or frozen English peas, 1½ cups (about 7 oz/220 g)

Sugar snap peas, 6 oz (185 g), strings removed

Gluten-free chicken broth, 1 cup (8 fl oz/250 ml)

Fresh mint, 2 tablespoons minced

Fresh lemon juice, 1½ tablespoons

MAKES 2 SERVINGS; CAN BE DOUBLED

1 Spread the flour mix on a plate. Cut the chicken tenders in half crosswise. Sprinkle the chicken lightly with salt and pepper, then dredge in the flour.

2 In a large nonstick frying pan over medium-high heat, warm the oil. Add the chicken and sauté until just cooked through, about 5 minutes. Transfer to a plate. Add the peas and sugar snaps to the frying pan and season lightly with salt and pepper. Sauté until heated through, about 2 minutes. Add the broth and bring to a boil, stirring up the browned bits on the pan bottom. Cover the pan and boil until the vegetables are almost tender, about 3 minutes.

3 Return the chicken and any juices on the plate to the pan. Add the mint and simmer uncovered until the sauce thickens and coats the chicken, stirring almost constantly, about 2 minutes. Stir in the lemon juice. Taste and adjust the seasoning. Divide the chicken and vegetables between 2 warmed plates and serve right away.

Better than grandmother's, this soup offers comfort in a bowl; I make it to ward off the flu or cheer myself up on a bad day. The quality of the broth will influence the dish so choose a flavorful, gluten-free broth.

Chicken and Rotelle Soup with Fresh Ginger and Basil

I use quinoa and corn rotelle for this. The texture is just right and the little squiggles fit nicely in soup spoons.

To mince ginger efficiently, remove the peel with a vegetable peeler, and then slice the ginger thinly. Fan out the slices like dominos, cut crosswise into thin strips, and finally cut across the strips to mince.

To slice basil, stack a handful of leaves on a cutting board and cut crosswise with a sharp knife.

Vegetable oil, 1 tablespoon

Yellow onion, 1, coarsely chopped

Fresh ginger, ⅓ cup (1½ oz/45 g) minced

Fresh shiitake mushrooms, 6–8 oz (185–250 g), stemmed and sliced

Low-sodium, gluten-free chicken broth, 8 cups (64 fl oz/2 l)

Skinless, boneless chicken thighs, 1 lb (500 g)

Gluten-free rotelle pasta, 4 oz (125 g)

Edamame, 1½ cups (about 9 oz/ 280 g) ready-to-eat shelled

Fresh lemon juice, 2 teaspoons

Kosher salt and freshly ground pepper

Green onions, 3, white and light green parts, sliced

Fresh basil leaves, about 1 cup (1.5 oz/40 g) thinly sliced

MAKES 4–6 SERVINGS

1 In a large pot over medium heat, warm the oil. Add the onion and ginger and sauté for 3 minutes to soften slightly. Add the mushrooms and sauté until the onion is translucent, about 2 minutes longer. Add the broth and 2 cups (16 fl oz/500 ml) water, increase the heat to high, and bring to a boil. Add the chicken and return the liquid to a boil. Reduce the heat to medium-low and simmer until the chicken is cooked through, about 8 minutes. Using tongs, transfer the chicken to a plate.

2 Add the rotelle to the pot, stir well, increase the heat to high and boil, stirring frequently, until the rotelle are almost tender, about 8 minutes. Meanwhile, cut the chicken into bite-sized pieces.

3 Add the chicken, edamame, and lemon juice to the soup and simmer until heated through. Season to taste with salt and pepper. Ladle the soup into warmed bowls. Sprinkle with green onions and basil and serve right away.

This dish was inspired by a visit to the central market in Oaxaca. Smoky grilled chicken and vegetables, a quick guacamole, and romaine tossed with a creamy dressing are ready for diners to create their own custom tacos.

Grilled Chicken, Pepper, and Zucchini Tacos

Olive oil, ¼ cup, plus 1 tablespoon

Smoked paprika, 4 teaspoons

Ground cumin, 1¼ teaspoon

Ground coriander, 1¼ teaspoon

Skinless, boneless chicken breast halves, ¾–1 lb (375–500 g), halved horizontally

Kosher salt and freshly ground pepper

Long, slender zucchini, 2, trimmed and quartered lengthwise

Poblano chiles, 2, quartered lengthwise, seeded

Large red bell pepper, 1, quartered lengthwise and seeded

Red onion, 1 large, halved through the stem end, then cut crosswise into slices ½ inch (12 mm) thick

Large romaine heart, 1, sliced crosswise

Fresh cilantro, 3 tablespoons chopped

Fresh lime juice, 1 teaspoon

Gluten-free mayonnaise, 1 tablespoon

Quick Guacamole (page 215)

Gluten-free corn tortillas, 8–12 (5½–6-inches/14–15 cm in diameter), warmed

MAKES 4 SERVINGS

Cutting the chicken breasts in half horizontally creates more surface area to absorb the cumin- and coriander-accented marinade.

1 In a small bowl, mix together ¼ cup (2 fl oz/60 ml) of the oil, the paprika, cumin, and coriander. Place the chicken on a small baking sheet and brush lightly on both sides with the oil mixture. Sprinkle with salt and pepper. Combine the zucchini, poblanos, bell pepper, and onion in a large bowl. Add the remaining oil mixture and toss to coat. Sprinkle with salt and pepper.

2 Prepare a grill for direct-heat cooking over high heat. Meanwhile, in a bowl, combine the lettuce, remaining 1 tablespoon oil, cilantro, lime juice, and mayonnaise and toss to blend. Season to taste with salt and pepper.

3 Place the vegetables on the grill rack, cover, and cook until browned and tender, about 6 minutes on each side. Transfer the vegetables to a platter. Add the chicken to the grill, cover, and cook until springy to the touch and cooked through, about 2½ minutes on each side. Cut the vegetables and chicken into thin strips and arrange on a warmed platter. Serve with the romaine, guacamole, and tortillas, allowing diners to fill tortillas with chicken and vegetables, then guacamole and lettuce.

With rich, toasty flavors and a tender crumb, no one will guess this loaf is gluten-free. I prepare it in a cast iron frying pan, which I can bring right to the table, and serve it warm with butter. For a satisfying breakfast, lunch, or snack, smear leftovers with peanut butter. Sometimes I make this loaf with ½ cup (4 fl oz/125 ml) maple syrup rather than the brown sugar, and mix it in with the liquid ingredients.

Skillet Cornbread

Gluten-free cornmeal, 1 cup
(5 oz/155 g) (I like Bob's Red Mill)

Gluten-free flour mix, 1 cup
(5 oz/155 g) (I like Cup4Cup)

Brown sugar, ⅓ cup (2½ oz/75 g),
firmly packed

Baking powder, 2½ teaspoons

Kosher salt, 1 teaspoon

Baking soda, ½ teaspoon

Xanthan gum, ¾ teaspoon (optional)

Freshly ground pepper

Additions of your choice such as
4 oz (125 g) shredded extra-sharp
Cheddar cheese; 2 teaspoons minced
jalapeño chiles; or 1 cup (6 oz/185 g)
corn kernels

Buttermilk, 1 cup

Large egg, 1

Butter, ½ cup (4 oz/125 g),
or 6 tablespoons olive oil

Fresh sage or rosemary,
1½ tablespoons minced (optional)

MAKES 1 LARGE LOAF

If using Cup4Cup flour mix, you won't need the xanthan gum, which is essential for binding most gluten-free baked goods.

If you like, multiply the ingredients in the recipe by 1½ times and divide among 4 miniature (6 inches/15 cm) cast iron pans (shown at left). The baking time is the same.

Preheat the oven to 400°F (200°C). Warm a 10-inch (25 cm) ovenproof frying pan, preferably cast iron, in the oven for 10 minutes. Meanwhile, in a large bowl, combine the cornmeal, flour mix, brown sugar, baking powder, salt, baking soda, xanthan gum (if you are NOT using Cup4Cup flour mix), and a generous amount of pepper. Whisk to blend and mix in any additions. In a small bowl, combine the buttermilk and egg and whisk to blend.

Using a pot holder, remove the frying from the oven. Add the butter and herbs, if using, and swirl until the butter melts and the herbs sizzle. Pour the butter into the buttermilk mixture, leaving just enough butter in the pan to coat it. Whisk to incorporate, and then add to the dry ingredients. Using a wooden spoon, stir just until combined. Spoon the batter into the skillet, spreading to cover evenly.

Using a pot holder, return the pan to the oven. Bake until the bread is brown and feels springy when pressed in the center, about 20 minutes. Let cool for at least 10 minutes. Serve warm or at room temperature.

Redolent of cumin, green chiles, and marjoram—my favorite underutilized herb—and thick and creamy from cannellini beans, this dish is easy to pull off on a weeknight, and also festive for a casual chili party.

Turkey and White Bean Chili

Olive oil, 1 tablespoon

Large yellow onion, 1, finely chopped

Large red bell pepper, 1, chopped

Large clove garlic, 1, minced (optional)

Red pepper flakes, ½ teaspoon

Ground cumin, 2 teaspoons

Ground dark-meat turkey, 1 lb (500 g)

Kosher salt and freshly ground black pepper

Cannellini beans, 2 cans (15 oz/470 g each), liquid drained and reserved

Gluten-free chicken broth, 1 cup (8 fl oz/250 ml)

Diced green chilies, 2 cans (4 oz/145 g each)

Heavy cream, ⅓ cup (3 fl oz/80 ml)

Dried marjoram, 1 teaspoon

Fresh cilantro, coarsely chopped for garnish

Toppings of your choice such as finely chopped red onion, minced red jalapeño, diced peeled avocado

MAKES 4–6 SERVINGS

Mash together any leftover condiments for an instant guacamole-like spread. I enjoy it as a satisfying snack or appetizer on rice crackers.

I always serve Skillet Cornbread (page 139) on the side, but corn tortillas are good, too.

1 In a heavy large pot over medium-high heat, warm the oil. Add the onion, bell pepper, garlic, if using, and pepper flakes and sauté until the onion is translucent, about 8 minutes. Add the cumin and stir until fragrant, about 30 seconds. Add the turkey and sprinkle lightly with salt and black pepper. Cook until the turkey is no longer pink, breaking up the meat with a spoon, about 4 minutes.

2 Add the beans and ⅔ cup (5 fl oz/160 ml) of their liquid to the pot along with the broth, green chiles, cream, and marjoram. Bring to a boil, stirring frequently. Reduce the heat and simmer to blend the flavors, stirring occasionally, about 15 minutes; thin with more bean liquid, if desired.

3 Taste the chili and adjust the seasoning. Spoon into warmed bowls and sprinkle with cilantro. Serve right away with the toppings in bowls alongside.

This brightly flavored sauce is naturally gluten-free, and the accompanying quinoa is great for absorbing the juices. I love to cook chicken and fish this way, too, and top them with the chunky sauce.

Turkey Cutlets with Green Olives and Lemon

Pimento-stuffed green olives, ¾ cup (4 oz/125 g) chopped

Fresh flat-leaf parsley, ¼ cup (¼ oz/8 g) minced

Finely grated lemon zest, 1½ teaspoons

Turkey breast cutlets, 1½ lb (750 g)

Kosher salt and freshly ground pepper

Sweet paprika, 1½ teaspoons

Ground cumin, 1½ teaspoons

Olive oil, 2 tablespoons, plus more if needed

Red onion, ¾ cup (4 oz/125 g) minced

Red pepper flakes (optional)

Fresh lemon juice, ¼ cup (2 fl oz/60 ml)

Gluten-free chicken broth, ¾ cup (6 fl oz/180 ml)

Extra-virgin olive oil, 2 tablespoons

Basic Quinoa (page 74)

MAKES 4 SERVINGS

Cooking the turkey over medium rather than medium-high heat turns out moist and tender meat without the need to protect it with a flour coating.

1 In a small bowl, combine the olives, parsley, and lemon zest. Sprinkle the turkey lightly on both sides with salt and pepper, and then sprinkle with the paprika and cumin.

2 In a large frying pan over medium heat, warm 1 tablespoon of the oil. In batches, add the turkey and sauté until browned and just cooked through, 1–3 minutes per side, depending on thickness of the meat, and adding more oil to the pan if needed. Transfer the cooked turkey to a warmed platter and tent with foil to keep warm.

3 In the same frying pan over medium heat, warm 1 tablespoon oil. Add the onion and a pinch of pepper flakes, if using, and sauté for 1 minute. Add the lemon juice and bring to a boil, scraping up any browned bits. Add the olive mixture and broth. Boil until the liquid is syrupy, about 2 minutes. Mix in any juices on the turkey platter and the 2 tablespoons extra-virgin olive oil. Season to taste with salt and pepper.

4 Divide the quinoa among 4 warmed plates, then top with the turkey. Spoon the olive mixture and pan drippings over the turkey and serve right away.

The mint in our garden explodes in the early summer, and was the inspiration for this fresh-tasting dish. I grind the herb with toasted almonds and extra-virgin olive oil for a sauce that is also great with fish and lamb.

Chicken Cutlets and Carrots with Mint Pesto

Extra-virgin olive oil, 2 tablespoons

Chicken breast cutlets, ¾ lb (375 g)

Kosher salt and freshly ground black pepper

Shallot, 1, minced

Red pepper flakes

Carrots, 2, shredded (about 2¼ cups/6 oz/185 g)

Lemon Juice, 2 teaspoons

Mint Pesto (page 214)

Hot water, if needed

Fresh mint leaves, cut into thin slices for garnish

MAKES 2 SERVINGS

If you are really pressed for time, look for packaged shredded carrots at the market.

The pesto keeps well in the refrigerator, so make extra to use on another night.

1 In a large nonstick frying pan over medium-high heat, warm 1 tablespoon of the oil. Sprinkle the chicken with salt and pepper and add to the frying pan. Sauté until cooked through, 2–3 minutes per side. Transfer the chicken to a warmed plate.

2 Add the remaining 1 tablespoon oil to the same frying pan, and then add the shallot and a pinch of pepper flakes. Sauté until the shallot begins to soften, about 1 minute. Add the carrots and sprinkle lightly with salt and black pepper. Sauté until the carrots are tender-crisp, 2–3 minutes. Mix in the lemon juice and any juices from the plate holding the chicken. Taste and adjust the seasoning.

3 Divide the carrots between 2 warmed plates. Top with the chicken. Thin the pesto with a little hot water, if desired. Spoon the pesto over the chicken, sprinkle with sliced mint, and serve right away.

Vietnamese food is a favorite at my house, and inspired this slightly spicy dish, fragrant with lemongrass and fresh cilantro. Green beans tossed with sesame oil are a fitting accompaniment.

Grilled Lemongrass Chicken with Ginger Rice

Be careful to seek out gluten-free tamari, as some is made with wheat. You generally don't have to worry about Asian fish sauce, because most are naturally gluten-free.

To mince lemongrass, pull off the outer layers to reveal the tender white inner core. Slice thinly crosswise, and then chop. Use a heavy knife because lemongrass is very fibrous.

I like to make a double batch of the chicken, rice, and vegetables here and turn the leftovers into a rice salad the next day.

Shallot, 2 tablespoons minced

Gluten-free tamari, 2 tablespoons

Sugar, 1½ tablespoons

Asian fish sauce, 1½ tablespoons

Lemongrass stalks, 1 fat or 2 thin, peeled and minced, or 2 teaspoons grated lemon zest

Vegetable oil, 1 tablespoon

Asian chile sauce, ½ teaspoon (such as sambal oelek or Sriracha)

Kosher salt, ½ teaspoon

Skinless, boneless chicken thighs, 1½ pounds (750 g)

GINGER RICE

Fresh ginger, 1½ tablespoons minced

Kosher salt, ⅛ teaspoon

Uncooked brown basmati or jasmine rice, 1 cup (7 oz/220 g)

Gluten-free tamari, 2 teaspoons

Chopped green onions for garnish

MAKES 4 SERVINGS

1. In a bowl, mix the shallot, the 2 tablespoons tamari, sugar, fish sauce, lemongrass, oil, chile sauce, and salt. Cut any excess fat from the chicken. Add the chicken to the bowl and toss to coat. Let the chicken marinate while preparing the rice.

2. To make the ginger rice, in a small saucepan, bring 1½ cups (12 fl oz/375 ml) water, the ginger, and salt to a boil. Add the rice and return to a boil. Reduce the heat to low, cover, and cook for 30 minutes. Turn off the heat and let stand at least 5 minutes. Fluff the rice with a fork, then mix in the tamari.

3. Meanwhile, prepare a grill for direct-heat cooking over high heat. Remove the chicken from the marinade and add to the grill rack, cover, and cook until springy to the touch and cooked through, about 6 minutes per side.

4. Divide the rice among 4 warmed plates. Top with the chicken, sprinkle with green onions, and serve right away.

Meat

Serving beef, lamb, and pork on a weeknight is a wonderful treat. To ensure the meat has the best flavor and was raised and treated humanely, I try to buy all my meat from a quality butcher shop that sources its meat from small family farms.

About Meat

Using thin, quick-cooking cuts and savvy techniques, preparing meat-based dishes during the week can be an enjoyable task. To help maintain my healthy lifestyle, I choose lean cuts and don't overdo the portions, letting meat shine alongside the farmers' market produce that inspires all of my cooking.

Choosing meat

Whenever I cook beef, I like to use grass-fed, and knowing it has better nutrition than corn-fed beef makes it a good choice for weeknight meals. Naturally lean cuts of lamb are terrific alternatives to beef, and can lend its unique flavor to give dinners a fresh twist. If available, I choose young, grass-fed lamb, which has a sweet, fresh flavor. Pork is also a fine choice for healthful dinners. As with all my meat, I insist on buying pork from ranchers who raise their animals humanely, and I believe it is better for the environment and translates to a superior flavor in the meat.

For everyday cooking, I choose beef cuts that are trim and economical: top sirloin for stir-fries; or flank and skirt steak for grilling. New York steak is also a favorite, and, while it may be expensive, the serving sizes are moderate and its rich flavor and tender texture make it worth the indulgence. Beef tenderloin can also be pricey, but it is a boon to weeknight cooks, as it is easy and quick to cook and has a buttery texture.

Boneless leg of lamb is delicious when broiled and cooks quickly. I also enjoy using ground lamb for a new take on burgers.

Pork tenderloin is a favorite for roasting, and pork chops can be sautéed or grilled for the same satisfaction as steak, but for less money. I also like to cut boneless pork chops or cutlets from the loin into strips for stir-fry. Another pork product I always keep on hand is pancetta, an unsmoked, Italian-style bacon. Just a little bit goes a long way to add flavor and depth to dishes.

Sourcing quality meat

I encourage you to get to know a butcher at a high-quality butcher shop or meat counter, who can ensure quality and answer any questions you have. Many farmers' markets also offer quality beef, lamb, and pork, and you can often buy directly from the people who raised and fed the animals.

Take care when buying sausages

Some sausage makers use bread or another wheat-based filler for their sausages. Be sure to check the label—or ask the butcher—to ensure you are buying prepared meats that are free of gluten.

Working with meat

I serve meat only a few times per month; when I do, I use only the best. I like to bring meat to room temperature before cooking to ensure that it cooks evenly. This usually means that, as soon as I get home from my busy work day, I take meat out of the refrigerator. Thin cuts are usually ready to go within 30 minutes.

Working with meat

Most beef cuts for purchase have already been trimmed of fat, but some may still have a noticeable layer. A little fat helps the meat stay moist during cooking and can be easily removed with a sharp knife before serving.

If I'm cooking grain-fed lamb or meat from older animals, I like to cut off lamb fat completely to offset a somewhat gamy flavor.

Pork tenderloin has a thick membrane, called silver skin, attached. To remove it, insert a thin-bladed knife between the meat and membrane near the tapered end of the meat. Keep the edge tilted slightly up against the silver skin, and cut along its length to remove it. Today's pork is perfectly safe to eat when served medium rare. Overcooked pork will be dry.

Partially freezing raw meat

If your recipe calls for cutting meat into thin slices, it's easier to accomplish if the meat is partially frozen. Put the meat in the freezer for about 30 minutes to firm it slightly before cutting. Be sure to use a sharp knife to ease slicing.

Slicing cooked meats

If you are working with meat that has stringy muscle fibers, such as flank steak, skirt steak, or leg of lamb, it's important to cut it perpendicularly through the fibers to encourage tenderness.

Roasting tips

Roasting is a favorite technique for weeknight cooking, as it is mostly hands-off and I can cook other elements of the meal at the same time. Be sure to let roasted meats rest for a few minutes prior to slicing. You can use the time to make a quick pan sauce from the flavorful drippings.

Grilling tips

When setting up a grill for cooking meats, it is useful to leave a section of it free of coals. This creates a cooler area to where you can move food to help manage flare-ups, which are common when fat or an oil-based marinade hits the flames. If you have a gas grill, be sure to preheat it with the cover closed for 10–15 minutes before grilling.

Sautéing tips

I like to use high heat when sautéing or pan-frying meat so that it gains a dark, caramelized surface that contrasts nicely with the tender pink meat inside. Be sure to warm the pan sufficiently before adding the meat (I look for a wisp of smoke coming off the pan), and turn on your kitchen ventilation to curtail odors.

I was unwilling to give up Mu Shu Pork—a favorite Chinese restaurant dish—when I changed my diet, so I devised this simple, and versatile version. I sometimes substitute chicken breast for the pork.

Easy Mu Shu Pork

Boneless center-cut pork loin cutlets or boneless center-cut pork chops, ½ lb (250 g), fat trimmed

Gluten-free tamari, 3 tablespoons

Dry sherry or dry vermouth, 1 tablespoon

Cornstarch, 1 teaspoon

Fresh ginger, 1 teaspoon plus 1 tablespoon minced

Gluten-free hoisin sauce, 2 tablespoons

Asian sesame oil, 2 teaspoons

Vegetable oil, 3 tablespoons

Large eggs, 2

Kosher salt and freshly ground black pepper

Green onions, 1 bunch, white and pale green parts thinly sliced

Red pepper flakes, ¼ teaspoon

Shredded green cabbage, 1 package (1 lb/500 g)

Gluten-free tortillas, 8 (5½–6-inches/ 14–15 cm in diameter), warmed

MAKES 4 SERVINGS

1 Cut the pork across the grain into thin strips. In a bowl, mix the pork with 1 tablespoon of the tamari, the sherry, cornstarch, and 1 teaspoon of the ginger. In a small bowl, mix the hoisin sauce, 1 tablespoon of the tamari, 1 teaspoon of the sesame oil, and 1 tablespoon water. Set aside.

2 In a 12-inch (30-cm) nonstick frying pan over medium-high heat, warm 1 tablespoon of the vegetable oil. Beat the eggs with a pinch of salt, add to the pan, and let stand until puffy, about 30 seconds. Stir until the eggs are just set, about 30 seconds; transfer to a platter. Return the pan to the heat and add 1 tablespoon of the vegetable oil. Add the pork mixture and stir until cooked through, about 3 minutes; add to the platter with the eggs.

3 Return the pan to the heat and add the remaining 1 tablespoon vegetable oil and then the green onions, pepper flakes, and remaining 1 tablespoon ginger. Stir until fragrant, about 30 seconds. Add the cabbage, and sprinkle with salt and black pepper. Stir to coat with the oil. Add 2 tablespoons water, cover, and cook until the cabbage wilts, about 2 minutes. Add the egg and pork with any drippings, the remaining 1 tablespoon tamari and 1 teaspoon sesame oil, and stir until heated through. Transfer to a warmed platter or shallow bowl. Serve right away along with the hoisin mixture to spread on each tortilla before filling with the pork.

Gluten-free Smart and Delicious Fiber and Flax corn tortillas, made by La Tortilla Factory, are a good replacement for Mandarin pancakes, because their flavor is closer to the taste of wheat than most corn tortillas.

To warm the tortillas, wrap in barely damp paper towels, and then plastic wrap. Set on a plate and microwave on high for about 1 minute.

I created this quick braised dish on a cold winter night when the wind was howling around our house. Beef tenderloin cooks so quickly, I can make a stew in under 30 minutes, start to finish.

Beef, Carrot, and Edamame Stew with Dill and Lemon

Olive oil, 2 tablespoons

Beef tenderloin, 1 lb (500 g), cut into 1-inch (2.5 cm) cubes

Kosher salt and freshly ground pepper

Red onion, 1 large, cut into 1-inch (2.5 cm) pieces

Carrots, ½ lb (250 g), peeled, halved lengthwise, and then cut crosswise into 1½-inch (4 cm) pieces

Ground cumin, 1 teaspoon

Sweet paprika, 1 teaspoon

Gluten-free flour mix, 1 tablespoon (I like Cup4Cup)

Low-sodium, gluten-free beef broth, 2½ cups (20 fl oz/625 ml)

Tomato paste, 1 tablespoon

Gluten-free tamari, 1 tablespoon

Edamame, ¾ cup (about 4 oz/125 g) ready-to-eat shelled

Fresh dill, ¼ cup (½ oz/15 g), minced

Lemon zest, 1 teaspoon grated

MAKES 4 SERVINGS

My trick for enhancing a sauce that I didn't have the time to simmer for hours is to add gluten-free tamari for umami.

I like to serve stews such as this one with Quick Mashed Potatoes (page 214) or gluten-free rotelle pasta tossed with olive oil, salt, and pepper.

1 In a 12-inch (30 cm) nonstick frying pan over medium-high heat, warm 1 tablespoon of the oil. Sprinkle the beef lightly with salt and pepper, add to the frying pan, and cook until brown on all sides, about 6 minutes. Using tongs, transfer the meat to a plate.

2 Warm the remaining 1 tablespoon oil in the same frying pan. Add the onion and carrots and sprinkle lightly with salt and pepper. Sauté until beginning to brown, about 5 minutes. Add the cumin and paprika and sauté until fragrant, about 30 seconds. Add the flour mix and stir for 30 seconds. Gradually mix in the broth and then the tomato paste and tamari.

3 Cover the pan and simmer until the carrots are tender-crisp, about 8 minutes. Return the beef to the pan, add the edamame, and simmer until heated through, about 3 minutes. Mix in the dill and lemon zest. Season to taste with salt and pepper and serve right away.

Juicy flank steak, crisp fingerling potatoes, and a crunchy salad all benefit from the versatile cumin, shallot, cilantro, and lemon sauce. The herb-flecked mixture is also great on chicken and fish.

Grilled Steak and Fingerlings with Herb Salad

Cumin seeds and coriander seeds, 2¼ teaspoons *each*

Flank steak, 1½ lb (750 g)

Extra-virgin olive oil, ½ cup (4 fl oz/125 ml) plus more as needed

Kosher salt and freshly ground black pepper

Shallot, 3 tablespoons minced

Fresh lemon juice, 3 tablespoons

Fresh cilantro or flat-leaf parsley, ¼ cup (⅓ oz/10 g) minced

Sweet paprika, 2 teaspoons

Cayenne pepper, ¼ teaspoon

Fingerling potatoes, 1¼ lb (750 g), halved lengthwise and partially cooked

Baby salad greens, 4 oz (120 g) (about 4 cups)

Mixed fresh herb leaves, such as cilantro, flat-leaf parsley, and basil, ½ cup (½ oz/15 g)

MAKES 4 SERVINGS

Start off this recipe by partially cooking the potatoes in boiling water for 10 minutes. This helps to prepare them to grill right along with the meat.

I like a mixture of flat-leaf parsley, cilantro, and basil in this salad.

1   In a small frying pan over medium heat, toast the cumin and coriander seeds, shaking frequently, until fragrant and starting to brown, about 1 minute. Grind the seeds coarsely in a mortar with a pestle. Place the steak on a baking sheet and brush on both sides with olive oil. Sprinkle with half of the seeds, and then season generously with salt and black pepper.

2   In a bowl, combine the ½ cup (4 fl oz/125 ml) olive oil, shallot, lemon juice, minced cilantro, paprika, cayenne pepper, and the remaining ground seeds to make a sauce. Season to taste with salt and black pepper. In another bowl, toss the potatoes with about 1 tablespoon oil and salt and pepper to taste.

3   Prepare a grill for direct-heat cooking over high heat. Place the steak on the grill rack. Arrange the potatoes cut side down on the grill rack. Cook the steak to the desired doneness, about 5 minutes per side for medium-rare. Grill the potatoes until golden brown on the cut side, about 5 minutes. Transfer the steak to a cutting board and let stand for 5 minutes.

4   Combine the greens, herb leaves, and 2–3 tablespoons of the sauce and toss to coat. Season to taste with salt and pepper. Slice the meat thinly across the grain, and arrange on plates with the potatoes and salad. Serve right away, passing the remaining sauce at the table.

Here, a juicy burger is topped with a big serving of Greek salad. Mint-scented quinoa stands in for a bun to absorb the yummy flavors. I make this with a sheep's milk feta cheese, which lends a wonderful fresh taste.

Lamb Burgers with Mint Greek Salad Topping

Quinoa, 1 cup (8 oz/250 g)

Kosher salt, 1 teaspoon, plus more as needed

Large plum tomatoes, 10 oz (315 g), halved and seeded, then finely diced

Persian cucumber, 1, finely diced

Feta cheese, 3 tablespoons diced

Red onion, ½ cup (2½ oz/80 g), plus 2 tablespoons finely chopped

Fresh mint, ½ cup (¾ oz/20 g), chopped

Ground lamb, 1¼ lb (625 g)

Sweet paprika, 1½ teaspoons

Freshly ground pepper

Extra-virgin olive oil, 1 tablespoon, plus more as needed

MAKES 4 SERVINGS

Make an indentation with your thumb in the center on one side of the meat patties to help them stay flat during cooking. Without this step, they tend to swell up into a tennis ball shape.

1 Rinse and drain the quinoa 4 times, then place in a saucepan. Add 1½ cups (12 fl oz/375 ml) water and a pinch of salt and bring to a boil. Reduce the heat to low, cover, and simmer until all the water is absorbed, about 15 minutes. Turn off the heat and let stand at least 5 minutes.

2 In a small bowl, mix the tomatoes, cucumber, cheese, 2 tablespoons of the onion, and 2 tablespoons of the mint. Season to taste with salt and pepper.

3 In a bowl, combine the ground lamb, paprika, remaining ½ cup (2½ oz/77 g) onion, ¼ cup (⅓ oz/10 g) of the mint, 1 teaspoon salt, and a few grinds of pepper; mix gently to blend. Form the lamb mixture into 4 patties, each ½ inch (12 mm) thick. Using your thumb, make an indentation in the center of each patty. Sprinkle with salt and pepper. Heat a large frying pan over medium-high heat; brush with oil. Add the patties to the pan and cook until done to your liking, about 3 minutes per side for medium-rare.

4 Fluff the quinoa with a fork. Mix in the 1 tablespoon oil and the remaining 2 tablespoons mint. Season to taste with salt and pepper. Divide the quinoa among 4 warmed plates and top each with a lamb patty. Spoon the tomato mixture generously over the patties and quinoa and serve right away.

I find it comforting to stir up a sweet-smelling risotto while I exchange work stories with my husband at the end of the day. This one includes both vegetables and meat, so it's not necessary to prepare another dish.

Sausage and Chard Risotto

Low-sodium, gluten-free chicken broth, 4 cups (32 fl oz/1 l)

Olive oil, 1 tablespoon

Yellow onion, 1, chopped

Gluten-free Italian sausage, ½ lb (250 g), preferably spicy, casings removed

Fresh rosemary, 1 teaspoon minced

Arborio rice, 1½ cups (14 oz/440 g)

Dry vermouth or dry white wine, ½ cup (4 fl oz/125 ml)

Chard, 1 bunch, stems removed, leaves thinly sliced

Parmesan cheese, ½ cup (2 oz/60 g) freshly grated

Kosher salt and freshly ground pepper

MAKES 4 SERVINGS

Choose pork or turkey sausage for this versatile dish; just make certain it includes no wheat filler.

I prefer to use Swiss chard with white ribs for this recipe. Red chard tints the rice a pink hue.

1 In a saucepan, bring the broth and 1 cup (8 fl oz/250 ml) water to a simmer. Reduce the heat to low and keep warm while you are making the risotto.

2 In a heavy saucepan over medium-high heat, warm the oil. Add the onion and cook, stirring frequently, until nearly translucent, about 4 minutes. Add the sausage and rosemary and cook, breaking up the meat with a spoon, until it is no longer pink, about 4 minutes. Add the rice and stir until the rice is opaque, about 1 minute. Add the vermouth and cook, stirring, until it is absorbed, about 1 minute.

3 Add about ¾ cup (6 fl oz/180 ml) of the broth to the pan and adjust the heat so the liquid bubbles and is absorbed slowly. Cook, stirring frequently, until the liquid is absorbed. Continue to cook, adding the broth about ¾ cup at a time and stirring frequently, until the rice is almost tender but still slightly firm, about 15 minutes. Add the chard and continue cooking, stirring almost constantly, adding the liquid about ½ cup (4 fl oz/125 ml) at a time, until the rice is just tender but slightly firm in the center and the mixture is creamy, about 5 minutes longer.

4 Remove the risotto from the heat. Stir in the cheese. Season to taste with salt and pepper. Spoon the risotto into warmed bowls and serve right away.

I have always loved potatoes, but since switching to a gluten-free lifestyle, I have been enjoying them more and more to replace the satisfaction I used to get from wheat-based bread and pasta. One of my favorite ways to enjoy buttery Yukon golds is quickly steamed and then smashed with a spoon and mixed with fresh herbs or green onions, a little olive oil, and broth.

Smashed Potatoes with Herbs

Yukon gold potatoes, 1½ lb (750 g), unpeeled, cut into ½–¾ inch (12 mm–2 cm) pieces

Extra-virgin olive oil, 3 tablespoons

Gluten-free chicken broth, about ½ cup (4 fl oz/125 ml)

Fresh herbs or green onions, 2–4 tablespoons minced

Kosher salt and freshly ground black pepper

MAKES 4 SERVINGS

Steam the potatoes over simmering water until very tender, 15–18 minutes.

In a large nonstick frying pan over low heat, warm the oil. Add the potatoes. Using a wooden spoon, smash the potatoes coarsely, adjusting their texture as necessary with the broth. Mix in the herbs. Season to taste with salt and pepper and serve right away.

Change the flavoring depending on what the potatoes will be accompanying:

Basil goes well with Italian or Mediterranean flavor profiles

Cilantro goes well with Latin or Asian flavor profiles

Dill goes well with mustard, olives, capers, and most seafood or poultry

Flat-leaf parsley or chives are all-purpose herbs that can add freshness to any dish

Rosemary goes well with steaks and chicken (add it to the oil in the pan before smashing the potatoes)

Green onions are also great all-purpose flavorings for potatoes

Potatoes play an important role in the gluten-free diet, as in this recipe. Thin slices of steak are served over potatoes redolent of fresh rosemary, and then topped with barely warmed fresh tomatoes.

Pan-Fried Steak, Rosemary Potatoes, and Tomato Relish

New York strip steaks, 2
(12 oz/375 g each)

Kosher salt and freshly ground pepper

Minced fresh rosemary,
1½ tablespoons

Extra-virgin olive oil, 1½ tablespoons,
plus more as needed

Cherry or plum tomatoes,
12 oz (375 g), halved or diced

Fresh basil, ⅓ cup (½ oz/15 g) minced

Red onion, 3 tablespoons minced

Balsamic vinegar, 1½ teaspoons

Smashed Potatoes with Herbs
(page 165), using 2 tablespoons
rosemary

MAKES 4 SERVINGS

For fuller flavor, meaty plum tomatoes can be replaced with 1½ pounds (750 g) firm and slightly underripe heirloom tomatoes.

I like to steam potatoes for the smashed potatoes while I put together the ingredients for the relish. Then, I crush the potatoes and keep them warm in a covered frying pan while cooking the meat.

1   Place the steaks on a plate and season generously with salt and pepper. Press the rosemary into each side of each steak. Brush with olive oil. Let stand while preparing the relish.

2   In a small bowl, combine the tomatoes, basil, onion, vinegar, and 1½ tablespoons oil. Season to taste with salt and pepper.

3   Warm a heavy large frying pan over high heat. Add the steaks and cook as desired, 3–4 minutes on each side for medium-rare. Transfer the steaks to a cutting board. Add the tomato mixture to the frying pan and cook until just heated through, stirring up any browned bits, about 1 minute.

4   Slice the steaks across the grain and divide among 4 warmed plates. Spoon the tomato relish over the top. Spoon the smashed potatoes alongside and serve right away.

In just a few minutes, tender meat is cooked in a creamy-spicy sauce. Fresh herbs and lime juice are added just before serving to bring the flavors to life. Try this same recipe with shrimp or cubes of fish.

Thai-Style Beef and Broccoli Curry

Tenderloin is as tender as the name implies, and only a small amount is used here. However, it can be replaced with more economical top sirloin if you slice the meat very thinly to offset its chewiness.

When boiled, coconut milk thickens to a luxurious texture and is a pleasing replacement for flour-thickened sauces.

Broccoli florets, ¾ lb (375 g) (1½-inch/4 cm florets)

Vegetable oil, 1 tablespoon

Beef tenderloin, ¾ lb (375 g), trimmed, cut across the grain into thin slices

Kosher salt and freshly ground pepper

Large shallots, 2, sliced

Fresh ginger, 3 tablespoons minced

Thai red curry paste, 1 tablespoon

Coconut milk, 1 can (about 14 oz/ 440 g), stirred thoroughly

Brown sugar, 1 tablespoon

Asian fish sauce, 1 tablespoon

Brown jasmine or basmati rice (page 214)

Fresh basil leaves, ½ cup (½ oz/15 g) sliced

Lime wedges for serving

MAKES 4 SERVINGS

1 In a microwave-proof bowl, place the broccoli and 2 tablespoons water. Cover and cook in the microwave on high until the broccoli is just tender-crisp, 3–4 minutes.

2 In large nonstick frying pan over medium-high heat, warm the oil. Sprinkle the beef slices lightly with salt and pepper. Cook the beef in batches (do not crowd the pan) until just brown, about 1 minute on each side. Transfer the meat to a plate. Add the shallots and ginger and sauté until fragrant, about 1 minute. Add the curry paste and stir for 2 minutes. Add the coconut milk, sugar, and fish sauce and simmer until the sauce thickens, stirring up browned bits, about 2 minutes. Add the broccoli and beef and simmer until heated through.

3 Fluff the rice with a fork and then divide among 4 warmed bowls. Top with the beef-broccoli mixture. Sprinkle with basil and serve with lime wedges to squeeze over the top.

Boneless leg of lamb cooks to a juicy finish in about 8 minutes per side under a hot broiler. Chickpeas, tossed with carrots and some colorful radicchio, absorb the lamb drippings even better than crusty bread.

Lamb with Chickpea, Carrot, and Radicchio Sauté

Shallots, 2, minced

Lemon zest, 2 tablespoons grated

Fresh rosemary, 1 tablespoon minced

Boneless leg of lamb, 1¼–1½ lb (625–750 g), most of the fat trimmed

Olive oil, 2 tablespoons, plus more as needed

Kosher salt and freshly ground pepper

Carrots, 4, halved lengthwise and sliced

Chickpeas, 1 can (15 oz/470 g), rinsed and drained

Radicchio, 1 head, quartered, cored, and then sliced

Dry vermouth or dry white wine, ⅓ cup (3 fl oz/80 ml)

Gluten-free chicken broth, ⅓ cup (3 fl oz/80 ml)

Fresh lemon juice, 1 tablespoon

MAKES 4 SERVINGS

I have discovered that organic chickpeas are more tender than standard, and I always keep a few cans in my cupboard for soups, stews, and hummus.

If you don't have a broiler pan, use a rack set over a rimmed baking sheet.

1 Position the oven rack so the meat will be 4 inches from the heat source and preheat the broiler. Meanwhile, in a small bowl, mix 3 tablespoons of the shallots, the lemon zest, and rosemary. Place the lamb on a broiler pan, brush all over with oil, and sprinkle generously with salt and pepper. Rub 1½ tablespoons of the shallot-lemon mixture into each side of the lamb. Broil the lamb until a thermometer inserted in the thickest part registers 130°–135°F (54°–57°C) for medium-rare, about 8 minutes per side. Transfer to a warmed platter and tent loosely with foil. Set the pan aside.

2 In a heavy large frying pan over medium heat, warm the 2 tablespoons oil. Add the remaining shallots and the carrots and sauté until beginning to soften, about 3 minutes. Add the chickpeas and sauté for 3 minutes. Add the radicchio and remaining shallot-lemon mixture and sauté until the radicchio starts to wilt, about 2 minutes.

3 Set the bottom part of the broiler pan on the stove top over medium heat. Add the vermouth and bring to a boil, stirring up the browned bits. Add to the chickpeas and boil until the liquid is reduced by half. Add the broth and simmer until almost absorbed, about 3 minutes. Mix in the lemon juice and any juices on the platter. Season to taste with salt and pepper. Slice the meat thinly across the grain and serve right away with the chickpea mixture.

Based on the Vietnamese dish *pho,* this recipe features fragrant broth, supple rice noodles, thin steak slices, and fresh herbs for a complete meal. I make this, or a chicken version, two or three times a month.

Quick Vietnamese Beef and Noodle Soup

Vegetable oil, 1 tablespoon

Yellow onion, 1, coarsely chopped

Fresh ginger, 3 tablespoons minced

Low-sodium, gluten-free beef broth, 8 cups (64 fl oz/2 l)

Asian fish sauce, 2 tablespoons

Sugar, 1 tablespoon

Star anise pods, 10

Whole cloves, 6

Pad Thai rice noodles, 8–10 oz (215–315 g)

Thai chiles, 6, or 1 serrano chile, thinly sliced with seeds

Bean sprouts, fresh basil sprigs, and lime wedges for serving

New York strip steak, ½–¾ lb (265–375 g), partially frozen (page 152)

Green onions, 3, thinly sliced

Chopped fresh cilantro, ⅓ cup (½ oz/15 g)

Freshly ground black pepper

MAKES 4 SERVINGS

Look for rice noodles that are ¹⁄₁₆ inch (2 mm) wide and are shaped like linguine. They will increase in width when cooked.

Partially freezing the steak makes it easy to slice into thin pieces, which then cook quickly when the hot broth is poured over the top.

1 In a large pot over medium heat, warm the oil. Add the chopped onion and ginger and sauté until the onion is translucent, about 5 minutes. Add the broth, 2 cups (16 fl oz/8 ml) water, the fish sauce, and sugar. Place the star anise and cloves in a tea strainer or wrap in cheesecloth and add to the pot. Bring to a boil. Reduce the heat to low and simmer for 30 minutes to develop the flavors.

2 Meanwhile, prepare the accompaniments: Place the noodles in a large heatproof bowl. Cover with boiling water and let soak 8 minutes to soften. Drain the noodles. Place the chiles, sprouts, basil sprigs, and lime wedges on a platter or in small bowls and set them on the table. Cut the steak in half lengthwise and trim off the fat. Slice it across the grain as thinly as possible.

3 Just before serving, remove the spices from the broth, add the noodles, and simmer for 2 minutes. Using tongs, divide the noodles among 4 warmed deep bowls. Place the steak atop the noodles, arranging it in a single layer. Ladle the simmering broth over the steak. Sprinkle the green onions, cilantro, and a few grinds of black pepper atop each bowl. Serve right away, allowing diners to add the chiles, sprouts, herbs, and lime juice to taste.

To enjoy this dish in the Korean style, place a mound of rice in a lettuce leaf (which is a refreshing gluten-free wrapper that you could use for any filling), top with a bite of meat, and a little slaw. Fold and eat it like a taco.

Grilled Korean-Style Short Ribs with Asian Slaw

The quick marinating time suggested here is sufficient, but the meat will have greater depth of flavor if you can marinate it overnight.

Ask the butcher to cut flanken-style beef short ribs across the bones into slices ⅓–½ inch (9–12 mm) thick.

Gluten-free tamari, ⅔ cup (5 fl oz/160 ml)

Green onions, 8, chopped

Brown sugar, 6 tablespoons (3 fl oz/90 ml)

Rice vinegar, ¼ cup (2 fl oz/60 ml)

Asian sesame oil, 3 tablespoons

Shallots, 2 tablespoons minced

Fresh ginger, 2 tablespoons minced

Asian chile paste such as sambal oelek, ½ teaspoon

Korean-style short ribs, 3 lb (1.5 kg)

Asian Slaw (page 215)

Cooked short-grain brown rice

Red leaf lettuce (optional)

MAKES 4 SERVINGS

1 In a glass baking dish, combine the tamari, half of the green onions, the brown sugar, vinegar, sesame oil, shallots, ginger, and chile paste. Mix to blend. Add the meat and turn to coat. Let the meat marinate at room temperature while preparing the slaw and rice (or cover and refrigerate the marinating meat overnight).

2 Prepare a grill for direct-heat cooking over high heat. Remove the meat from the marinade and place on the grill rack. Cook to the desired doneness, about 3 minutes per side for medium-rare. Transfer the short ribs to a platter. Sprinkle with the remaining chopped green onions and serve right away with the slaw, rice, and lettuce leaves, if using.

We hosted two exchange students from China last summer, and noodles made them happier than anything else I cooked during their three-week stay. Here is the dish we came up with together for a dinner party.

Chinese-Style Peanut Noodles with Seared Beef

Boneless beef top sirloin, ¾ lb (375 g), trimmed, halved lengthwise, and partially frozen (page 152)

Gluten-free tamari, 5 tablespoons (3 fl oz/80 ml)

Sugar, 1¾ teaspoons

Green onions, 4, minced

Asian sesame oil, 1½ teaspoons plus 2 tablespoons

Kosher salt and freshly ground pepper

Creamy old fashioned–style peanut butter, ⅓ cup (4 oz/125 g)

Fresh ginger, 2 tablespoons minced

Balsamic vinegar, 2 tablespoons

Red pepper flakes, ½ teaspoon

Gluten-free spaghetti, 10 oz (315 g) (I like Schar)

Large red bell pepper, 1, halved lengthwise and seeded, then halved crosswise and cut into very thin slices

Vegetable oil, 1 tablespoon

Fresh cilantro, ¼ cup chopped

MAKES 4 SERVINGS

Snow peas or sugar snaps can replace the bell pepper here. Start with 8 oz (250 g), cut them lengthwise into thin strips, and cook along with the pasta during the last 3 minutes.

You can also make this dish with chicken. Either way, it is a great one to bring to a potluck to ensure there is a gluten-free dish for you to eat.

1   Cut the beef across the grain into ¼-inch (6-mm) slices. In a bowl, combine 2 tablespoons of the tamari and ¾ teaspoon of the sugar and stir to dissolve. Mix in half of the green onions, 1½ teaspoons of the sesame oil, and a generous amount of black pepper. Add the beef and stir to coat. Set aside.

2   In a food processor, combine the peanut butter, ginger, vinegar, pepper flakes, remaining 3 tablespoons tamari, remaining green onions, 1 tablespoon of the sesame oil, and 1 teaspoon of the sugar. Add ¼ cup (2 fl oz/60 ml) hot water and process until well blended to make a sauce.

3   Add the spaghetti to a large pot of boiling salted water and stir well. Cook, stirring frequently, until al dente, about 8 minutes. Drain, rinse briefly with cold water, and drain well. Place in a warmed bowl. Add the remaining 1 tablespoon sesame oil and stir to coat. Mix in the bell pepper and sauce to taste. Mix to coat the noodles, then season to taste with salt and pepper.

4   In a heavy large frying pan over high heat, warm the vegetable oil. Working in batches, sear the beef in a single layer, about 20 seconds on each side. Transfer to a cutting board and halve each piece lengthwise. Divide the noodles among 4 bowls, top with the beef, sprinkle with cilantro, and serve.

This meal can be quickly assembled on a busy night and doubles as a picnic. Look for artisanal cured meats, or salumi, at specialty food stores and some markets. Serve with Soft Socca (page 26) or gluten-free crackers.

Salumi and Cheese with Fennel-Apple Salad

Gluten-free Dijon mustard, 1 tablespoon

Fresh lemon juice, 1 tablespoon

Extra-virgin olive oil, 3 tablespoons

Fresh mint, 2 tablespoons minced

Fennel seed, ¼ teaspoon

Kosher salt and freshly ground pepper

Large fennel bulb, 1

Large Jonathan or Pippin apple, 1

Baby arugula, 2 cups (2 oz/60 g)

Thinly sliced cured meats, such as salami, prosciutto, and speck, 6–8 oz (185–250 g)

Cheeses of your choice, 6 oz (185 g) total

Cherry tomatoes

Cured olives

MAKES 4 SERVINGS

When serving salami, be certain to check that it is gluten-free; some are made with wheat-based fillers.

1 In a small bowl, mix together the mustard and lemon juice. Gradually whisk in the olive oil to make a dressing. Add the mint and fennel seed, and then season to taste with salt and pepper to make a dressing.

2 Trim the fennel bulb, and then cut it lengthwise into quarters. Cut out the core, and cut crosswise into thin slices. Place in a bowl. Cut the apple into quarters and cut out the core. Cut into thin slices and add to the bowl with the fennel. Add the dressing and toss to coat. Season to taste.

3 Line a platter with the arugula. Mound the fennel-apple salad in the center of the platter. Arrange the cured meats, cheeses, tomatoes, and olives around the salad and serve right away.

This was inspired by the grilled ham and cheddar cheese sandwiches we served at lunch at one of my first cooking jobs in Weston, Vermont. Of course, there is no bread here, but freshly toasted corn tortillas instead.

Sausage-Pepper Quesadillas with Spinach-Apple Salad

Fresh lime juice, 1 tablespoon

Sweet paprika, ⅛ teaspoon

Olive oil, 3 tablespoons, plus more as needed

Green onion, 2 tablespoons minced

Fresh cilantro, 2 tablespoons minced

Sugar, 2 pinches

Kosher salt and freshly ground pepper

Baby spinach, 4 oz (125 g) (about 4 cups lightly packed)

Red-skinned apple, 1, quartered, cored, and thinly sliced

Gluten-free andouille sausage, 3–4 oz (90–125 g), halved lengthwise and thinly sliced crosswise

Large red bell pepper, ½, seeded and finely chopped

Gluten-free corn tortillas, 6 (5½–6-inches/14–15 cm in diameter)

Coarsely shredded sharp Cheddar or Manchego cheese, 1½ cups lightly packed (about 3 oz/90 g)

MAKES 2 SERVINGS; CAN BE DOUBLED

1 In a small bowl, whisk together the lime juice, paprika, and 3 tablespoons oil. Mix in the onion, cilantro, and sugar to make a dressing, then season to taste with salt and pepper. In a salad bowl, combine the spinach and apple.

2 Brush a large nonstick frying pan with olive oil and warm over medium-high heat. Add the sausage and sauté until beginning to brown, about 2 minutes. Transfer to a small bowl. Add the red pepper and sauté until tender and starting to brown, about 5 minutes. Transfer to another small bowl.

3 Heat a griddle or large frying pan over medium-low heat. Brush with olive oil. Add 2 tortillas and cook until softened slightly, about 30 seconds. Turn over and sprinkle 2 tablespoons of the cheese over half of each tortilla, leaving a border. Top with 1 tablespoon of the sausage and 1 tablespoon of the bell pepper. Sprinkle with 2 tablespoons of the cheese. Fold the empty side of the tortillas over the filling and press slightly. Cook until light golden and crisp, 2–3 minutes on each side. Transfer to warmed plates. Repeat with the remaining tortillas, cheese, sausage, and bell pepper, adding oil as needed.

4 Dress the salad to your liking and toss to coat the leaves. Serve right away with the quesadillas.

If you are doubling the recipe, keep the first batch of quesadillas warm on the lowest oven setting.

Since going gluten-free, I love to wrap almost anything in gently toasted corn tortillas, like the spice-rubbed steak and peppers here. The steak can also be grilled or replaced with chicken breast or strips of boneless pork.

Steak and Rajas Tacos

To toast tortillas, place them, one at a time, directly over a gas burner or in a hot skillet and cook until the aroma of toasted corn fills the air and the tortilla is beginning to brown, just a few seconds on each side. When I am toasting a big batch, I get two burners going and place the tortillas in a tortilla warmer or wrap them in foil so they stay hot.

Coriander seeds, 1 tablespoon crushed, or 2 teaspoons ground coriander

Cumin, 1 teaspoon ground

Ancho chile powder, 1 teaspoon

Skirt steak, about 1½ lb (750 g), cut crosswise into 3–4 inch (7.5–10 cm) lengths

Kosher salt and freshly ground pepper

Olive oil, 2½ tablespoons

Large red bell peppers, 2, halved lengthwise and crosswise, and then thinly sliced

Poblano chiles, 2, halved lengthwise and crosswise, and then thinly sliced

Large red onion, 1, halved and thinly sliced

Heavy cream or gluten-free beef broth, ¼ cup (2 fl oz/60 ml)

Fresh cilantro, ¼ cup (⅓ oz/10 g) minced

Large avocado, 1, sliced

Gluten-free corn tortillas, 8–12 (5½–6 inches/14–15 cm in diameter), warmed

MAKES 4 SERVINGS

1 In a small bowl, mix the coriander, cumin, and chile powder. Sprinkle the steak pieces on both sides with half of the spice mixture and generously with salt and pepper.

2 In a large nonstick frying pan over medium-high heat, warm 1½ tablespoons of the oil. Add the bell peppers, poblano chiles, and onion. Sprinkle lightly with salt and pepper and sauté until the vegetables are almost tender, about 8 minutes. Transfer to a large bowl.

3 In the same frying pan over medium-high heat, warm the remaining 1 tablespoon oil. Add the steak and cook for 3–4 minutes per side for medium-rare. Transfer the steak to a cutting board. Return the pan to the heat and add the vegetable mixture, cream, and remaining spice mixture. Stir until heated through, scraping up any browned bits. Season to taste.

4 Arrange the vegetables on one side of a warmed platter. Slice the steak across the grain and arrange on the second side of the platter. Sprinkle the steak and vegetables with cilantro. Serve with the sliced avocado and tortillas, allowing diners to assemble their own tacos.

A honey-mustard vinaigrette lends bright flavors to both the meat and salad. Unlike lettuce salads, which need to be served as soon as they are made, kale benefits from being prepared ahead.

Sautéed Pork Chops with Kale Salad

Cider vinegar, ¼ cup (2 fl oz/60 ml)

Gluten-free Dijon mustard, 1 tablespoon plus 1 teaspoon

Honey, 1 tablespoon plus 1 teaspoon

Olive oil, ½ cup (4 fl oz/125 ml) plus 3 tablespoons

Kosher salt and freshly ground pepper

Black kale leaves, 4 cups (4 oz/125 g) thinly sliced (about 14 stalks with center ribs removed, from 1 large bunch)

Tart green apple such as Pippin, 1, cut into matchsticks

Center-cut loin pork chops, 4, each about 1¼ inch (3 cm) thick

Fresh thyme, 4 teaspoons minced

Dried marjoram, 2 teaspoons, crumbled

Shallot, 2 tablespoons minced

Dry vermouth, ½ cup (4 fl oz/125 ml)

MAKES 4 SERVINGS

1 In a small bowl, mix together the vinegar, mustard, and honey. Gradually mix in ½ cup (4 fl oz/125 ml) plus 2 tablespoons of the oil to make a dressing and season to taste with salt and pepper. In a large bowl, combine the kale and apple. Add ⅓ cup (3 fl oz/80 ml) of the dressing and toss to coat. Season to taste with salt and pepper. Let stand for at least 10 minutes before serving.

2 Lightly sprinkle the pork chops on both sides with salt and pepper, and then sprinkle with the thyme and marjoram.

3 In a heavy large skillet over high heat, warm the remaining 1 tablespoon oil. Add the pork chops and cook until lightly browned, 1–2 minutes per side. Reduce the heat to medium-low, cover, and cook until the meat feels firm but not hard when pressed and an instant-read thermometer registers 145°F (63°C), 3–4 minutes per side. Mound the kale on a platter and top with the pork chops. Let stand while you make the sauce.

4 Pour off all but 1 tablespoon fat from the pan. Set the pan over medium heat, add the shallot, and sauté until fragrant, about 30 seconds. Add the vermouth and bring to a boil, scraping up the browned bits on the pan bottom. Remove from the heat and mix in the remaining dressing to make a sauce. Season the sauce to taste, then spoon over the pork chops and serve.

To cut the kale efficiently, stack the leaves and cut them crosswise using a sharp knife.

If you have leftover salad, don't throw it away: Surprisingly, it is even good the next day.

Sweet potatoes are a healthy gluten-free starch. I like to serve them baked or mashed (page 214) with this dish.

Bursting with bright Asian-style flavors, this dish is reviving after a stressful day. Made from mung beans, Saifun noodles have a delightfully chewy texture, absorb flavors well, and are naturally gluten free.

Noodles with Pork, Shiitakes, and Green Onions

Saifun noodles, 1 package (5–6 oz/155–185 g)

Ground pork, 1 lb (500 g)

Green onions, 2 bunches, thinly sliced

Gluten-free tamari, ¼ cup (2 fl oz/60 ml) plus 1 tablespoon

Asian sesame oil, 4 teaspoons

Vegetable oil, 2 tablespoons

Fresh ginger, 2 tablespoons minced

Garlic cloves, 2, minced

Shiitake mushrooms, 8 oz (250 g), stemmed and diced

Asian chile paste such as sambal oelek, 1 teaspoon

Gluten-free chicken broth or water, ⅔ cup (5 fl oz/160 ml)

Kosher salt and freshly ground pepper

Chopped fresh cilantro

MAKES 4 SERVINGS

Saifun noodles are also called bean threads or cellophane noodles. Look for them where Asian ingredients are sold.

1 Place the noodles in a large heatproof bowl. Pour over 6 cups (48 fl oz/1.5 l) boiling water and let soak until elastic when gently pulled, 10–15 minutes. Drain the noodles. Using kitchen scissors, cut across the bunch of noodles about 3 times to shorten the strands.

2 In a bowl, combine the ground pork, half of the green onions, 1 tablespoon of the tamari, and 2 teaspoons of the sesame oil and mix gently to blend.

3 In a large nonstick frying pan over medium-high heat, warm the vegetable oil. Add the ginger and garlic and stir until fragrant, about 30 seconds. Add the mushrooms and stir until beginning to soften, about 2 minutes. Add the meat mixture and stir until no longer pink, about 2 minutes. Pour off any fat in the pan. Mix in remaining ¼ cup (2 fl oz/60 ml) tamari, 2 teaspoons sesame oil, the chile paste, and noodles. Stir for 1 minute to coat. Add the broth and remaining green onions and simmer, stirring frequently, until most of the liquid is absorbed, about 3 minutes. Season to taste with salt and pepper.

4 Divide the noodle mixture among 4 warmed plates. Sprinkle with cilantro and serve right away.

Desserts

When I feel like a little something sweet, I turn to seasonal fruit to satisfy my craving. Naturally gluten free, quick to prepare, and easy to vary, fruit is the perfect choice for my busy lifestyle.

About Fruit Desserts

Fresh fruit makes a great gluten-free dessert for weeknights. Growing up, my mother served a parade of fresh fruit after dinner: strawberries in the spring; berries and stone fruit in summer; grapes, apples, and pears in the fall; tangerines and oranges in the winter. Following are some of my favorite ideas.

Spring

Mix chopped crystallized ginger and brown sugar into Greek yogurt. Top with halved cherries and lightly toasted almonds.

Sauté apricot wedges with butter, sugar, and nutmeg until the fruit is tender. Serve over vanilla frozen yogurt or ice cream.

Mix hulled and sliced strawberries with a little sugar and fresh mint. Serve over lemon sorbet.

Summer

Slice pitted peaches and place in bowls. Top with whipped cream flavored with brown sugar, rum, and vanilla extract.

Cut ripe cantaloupe or honeydew into bite-sized pieces. Sprinkle with fresh mint and a splash of Port or Marsala.

Cut plums into thin slices. Scrape in the seeds from a vanilla bean. Add sugar and toss. Serve topped with Greek yogurt or frozen yogurt.

Fall

Cut ripe pears into wedges and serve with San André cheese and toasted hazelnuts.

Cut apples into slices, then sauté with butter, brown sugar, and cinnamon until tender and glazed; spoon over vanilla frozen yogurt.

Cut ripe figs in half and arrange on plates. Top with Greek yogurt or mascarpone cheese mixed with honey and orange zest. Sprinkle with chopped toasted walnuts.

Winter

Arrange sliced peeled oranges on a platter. Drizzle with honey and sprinkle with cinnamon and lightly toasted almonds.

Mix chopped pineapple, brown sugar, and rum. Spoon over Greek yogurt or frozen yogurt.

Mix cut-up mango, kiwi, and banana with grated lime zest. Top with mango sorbet.

Roasting plums and other stone fruits intensifies flavors and brings out their juices. Here, crystallized ginger lends a spicy counterpoint in an easy syrup that is spooned over the fruit for serving.

Gingered Roasted Plums

Fresh plums, 4, halved and pitted (I like Santa Rosa plums)

Crystallized ginger, 2 tablespoons finely chopped

Sugar, 1 tablespoon

Greek-style yogurt or Sweetened Whipped Cream (page 215) for serving

MAKES 4 SERVINGS

I also like to use the ginger syrup with bowls of raspberries or strawberries spooned over Greek-style yogurt.

1   Preheat the oven to 400°F (200°C). Arrange the plums, cut-side down, on a small rimmed baking sheet. Roast until the plums are tender and their juices begin to emerge, about 10 minutes.

2   Meanwhile, in a small saucepan over medium heat, stir together the ginger, sugar, and 2 tablespoons water and bring to a gentle simmer. Cook until the flavors have blended and the liquid becomes lightly syrupy, about 5 minutes.

3   Divide the warm plums among small bowls. Drizzle with the ginger syrup, top with dollops of yogurt or whipped cream, and serve.

This chunky compote infused with Port and spices is perfect for a cool winter evening. It's great when you're craving something sweet on a weeknight, but it's also a wonderful last-minute dessert for unexpected guests.

Dried Fruits Simmered in Port

Mixed dried fruits, such as cranberries, figs, and apricots, 2 cups (12 oz/370 g)

Black peppercorns, 1 teaspoon

Port, 1 cup (8 fl oz/250 ml)

Sugar, ⅔ cup (5 oz/155 g)

Cinnamon sticks, 2

Greek-style yogurt or Sweetened Whipped Cream (page 215) for serving

MAKES 4–6 SERVINGS

Simmer the fruits as you begin your dinner prep. Set them aside while you eat and the compote will be ready when you finish the meal.

1 Cut any large dried fruits into bite-sized pieces. Put the peppercorns in a tea ball and place in a saucepan. Add the Port, sugar, and cinnamon sticks and bring to a simmer, stirring occasionally. Add the dried fruits and simmer for 5 minutes. Remove from the heat, cover, and set aside for at least 30 minutes to blend the flavors.

2 When ready to serve, remove the peppercorns and cinnamon stick. Divide among bowls, top with dollops of yogurt or whipped cream, and serve.

I always have bananas and dried coconut on hand, so this dish is easy to put together when I want a special treat. Don't skip the pinch of salt when making the sauce; it really helps bring out all the flavors.

Coconut-Rum Caramelized Bananas

Be sure to peel the bananas just before using; they tend to turn brown when exposed to the air.

Shredded dried coconut, ⅓ cup (1¼ oz/35 g)

Unsalted butter, 2 tablespoons

Light brown sugar, ½ cup (3½ oz/105 g) packed

Dark rum or water, 2 tablespoons

Kosher salt

Bananas, 4, peeled, halved crosswise, and quartered lengthwise

Vanilla ice cream for serving

MAKES 4 SERVINGS

1 Preheat the oven to 350°F (180°C). Spread the coconut on a rimmed baking sheet and toast in the oven, stirring occasionally, until lightly golden, about 5 minutes.

2 In a large frying pan over medium heat, melt the butter. Add the brown sugar and stir well. Add the rum and a pinch of salt and stir well. Add the banana pieces, cut side down, and reduce the heat to medium-low. Cook, turning once, until just tender and golden, about 5 minutes total.

3 Divide the bananas and sauce among dessert plates. Place a scoop of ice cream on each plate, top with the toasted coconut, and serve right away.

When you are in the mood for a hearty, comforting dessert, rice pudding is a great choice. It has all the satisfaction of flour-thickened stove-top pudding, but it is naturally gluten free. Enjoy it warm or cold.

Rice Pudding with Raisins

Milk, 3⅓ cups (27 fl oz/825 ml), or more as needed

Arborio rice, ⅔ cup (5 oz/155 g)

Golden raisins, ½ cup (3 oz/90 g)

Sugar, ½ cup (4 oz/125 g)

Kosher salt, ¼ teaspoon

Pure maple syrup, 3 tablespoons

Pure vanilla extract, 1 teaspoon

Freshly grated nutmeg

MAKES 6 SERVINGS

1 In a heavy saucepan over high heat, combine the milk, rice, raisins, sugar, and salt. Bring to a boil, stirring occasionally. Reduce the heat to low and cook, uncovered, stirring frequently, until the rice is tender and the mixture is thick, about 40 minutes.

2 Add the maple syrup, vanilla, and nutmeg to taste to the rice mixture. Stir to mix well.

3 To serve, spoon the hot pudding into bowls. Or, refrigerate the pudding for up to 2 days, thinning with milk, if needed, and serve cold.

If you don't have maple syrup on hand, substitute an equal amount of dark brown sugar.

If you enjoy crunchy desserts and sweets made with a pastry crust, it can be hard to find gluten-free sweets to satisfy your cravings. Meringues, made from egg whites and sugar, can stand in for cookies and crusts in a wide variety of dessert preparations. They take some time to put together and to bake, but they are a good weekend project and keep well for several days in an airtight container, ready for quick desserts during the week.

Meringues

Large egg whites, 2, at room temperature

Kosher salt

Cream of tartar, ¼ teaspoon

Superfine sugar, ¾ cup (3 oz/90 g)

Pure vanilla extract, ½ teaspoon

MAKES ABOUT 3 DOZEN COOKIES OR 12–16 DESSERT BASES

Preheat the oven to 275°F (135°C). Line 2 large rimmed baking sheets with parchment paper.

In a stand mixer fitted with the whisk attachment, combine the egg whites, a small pinch of salt, and the cream of tartar and whip on low speed until the salt and cream of tartar are dissolved and the mixture is foamy, about 1 minute. Increase the mixer speed to medium and continue to beat until the egg whites begin to thicken, 2–3 minutes. Increase the mixer speed to medium-high and beat until the egg whites form slightly bent peaks when you lift the whip.

Increase the mixer speed to high and slowly sprinkle in the sugar, beating the mixture for about 15 seconds after each addition. When all of the sugar has been added, continue to beat until the egg whites form stiff glossy peaks with tips that barely droop when the whip is raised, about 1 minute. Add the vanilla extract and beat well.

For Cookie-like Puffs

Spoon the mixture in dollops, using about 2 tablespoons for each puff, onto the prepared baking sheet, leaving a few inches between each one. Bake the meringues until lightly colored, about 30 minutes. Turn off the oven and prop open the oven door about 1 inch (2.5 cm). Let cool completely in the oven before serving, about 2 hours.

For Dessert Bases

Using a large spoon, drop about one-sixth of the mixture onto the prepared baking sheet. Using the back of the spoon and working in a circular motion, spread the dollop into a disk about 4 inches wide and make a depression in the center of each. Continue with the remaining meringue mixture. Bake the meringues until they are no longer tacky on the surface and are very lightly golden, about 1 hour. Turn off the oven and prop open the oven door about 1 inch (2.5 cm). Let cool completely in the oven before serving, about 2 hours.

———

Serve dessert bases as Pavlovas topped with ice cream, sorbet, whipped cream, sweetened Greek-style yogurt, sweetened fresh fruit, or a combination.

———

———

Fold 6 tablespoons (1½ oz/45 g) finely chopped toasted almonds, pistachios, or hazelnuts into the meringue before shaping and baking.

———

———

Fold 6 tablespoons (1½ oz/45 g) miniature chocolate chips or sweetened dried coconut into the meringue before shaping and baking.

———

Coconut macaroons are a naturally gluten-free cookie. If you like, dip the bottoms of the cookies into melted chocolate, return to the parchment-lined pan, and refrigerate until the chocolate is set.

Coconut Macaroons

To separate eggs, have ready 2 small bowls. Crack one egg and pull the shell halves apart. Gently pass the yolk back and forth between the shell halves, letting the white fall into one bowl. Put the yolk in the second bowl.

Be careful when separating egg whites for whipping. Even a speck of yolk hinders the process.

Large egg whites, 3, at room temperature

Cream of tartar, ¼ teaspoon

Kosher salt

Sugar, ¾ cup (6 oz/185 g)

Pure vanilla extract, ½ teaspoon

Gluten-free, sweetened shredded coconut, 4½ cups (10 oz/150 g)

MAKES ABOUT 48 COOKIES

1   Preheat the oven to 325°F (165°C). Line 3 baking sheets with parchment paper. In a large bowl, combine the egg whites and cream of tartar. Using a mixer on medium-high speed, beat until the egg whites are very foamy, about 1 minute. Add a pinch of salt. While beating continuously, gradually add the sugar and beat until stiff peaks form, 3–4 minutes.

2   Using a rubber spatula, stir in the vanilla. In 3 batches, gently fold the coconut into the beaten whites just until incorporated. Place rounded tablespoonfuls of the dough 1½ inches (4 cm) apart on the prepared baking sheets. Bake until the cookie edges begin to turn light golden brown, 19–22 minutes.

3   Let the cookies cool completely on the sheets, about 30 minutes. Store in a single layer in an airtight container at room temperature for up to 4 days.

I created this recipe for my wedding rehearsal dinner. They were gobbled up, and no one guessed they were gluten free. These keep for about a week and they also freeze well, so they're a good option for cookie lovers.

Ginger-Cherry Oatmeal Cookies

Unsalted butter, ¼ cup (2 oz/60 g), at room temperature

Brown sugar, ¾ cup (6 oz/185 g) packed

Granulated sugar, ¾ cup (6 oz/185 g)

Large eggs, 2

Baking soda, 1¼ teaspoons

Pure vanilla extract, 1 teaspoon

Kosher salt, ¼ teaspoon

Toasted almond butter, 1 cup (10 oz/310 g)

Gluten-free rolled oats, 3 cups (9 oz/180 g)

Crystallized ginger, ½ cup (3 oz/90 g) chopped

Dried cherries, ⅔ cup (3 oz/90 g)

MAKES ABOUT 48 COOKIES

The crystallized ginger and dried cherries can be replaced with coarsely chopped toasted almonds, raisins, and/or chocolate chips.

1 Preheat the oven to 350°F (180°C). Lightly butter cookie sheets. In the bowl of an electric mixer fitted with the paddle attachment, beat the butter until smooth. Add the brown sugar and granulated sugar and beat until well mixed. Add the eggs, baking soda, vanilla, and salt and beat until smooth. Add the almond butter and beat until smooth. Mix in the oats, ginger, and cherries.

2 Spoon the dough by rounded teaspoons and place on the prepared sheets, spacing them 2 inches (5 cm) apart. Bake until the cookies are light brown around the edges, about 12 minutes. Let them cool on the pans for minutes, then transfer to wire racks to cool completely. Store in an airtight container at room temperature for up to 1 week.

Gluten-Free Kitchen Savvy

Gluten is present in foods containing wheat, barley, rye, and malt, and also in processed foods or on kitchen tools and equipment used for preparing gluten-containing foods. Make a few changes to your kitchen set-up and shopping habits, and you'll discover that gluten-free eating is a simple task.

Prepare your kitchen

If not everyone in your household is gluten free, you'll want to protect yourself or your loved ones from accidental gluten contamination. First, set aside a dedicated cupboard in which only gluten-free products are stored. Next, reserve one or more cutting boards exclusively for non-gluten food prep (even a crumb from wheat bread can compromise the immune system of someone with a gluten sensitivity or allergy). Finally, depending on how severe the gluten sensitivity is in your household, you may wish to buy a separate set of tools and equipment to help avoid contact with gluten-containing ingredients. Consider a toaster (for toasting gluten-free bread); colanders (for draining gluten-free pasta); and other kitchen supplies and utensils, including sponges and dish towels in severe cases of gluten intolerance or celiac disease.

Focus on whole foods

I try to do as much of my shopping as possible at my local farmers' market, but there are always items I need to pick up at the grocery store. In general, I stick to the perimeter of the store—the produce section, dairy case, butcher shop, and seafood counter—where I find whole, unprocessed foods. I'll stroll down the pasta, canned goods, and snack aisles on my way to the check-out counter to pick up things like gluten-free pasta and grains, tomatoes, broths, and tortilla chips to round out the fresh foods. Despite the temptation, I avoid the bulk bin. Even if foods stored there are naturally gluten free, they can be cross-contaminated during the stocking process or by customers interacting with the food.

Read labels

I am always sure to give every label of processed food a close read, as gluten can sometimes be found in soups, bottled sauces, salad dressings, processed sliced meats, flavored nuts, broths, and many other types of things. Gluten is also sometimes added to naturally gluten-free processed foods to give it texture and savor. There are web sites that can tell you which processed foods are gluten free so you can save time while shopping.

Bring a dish to a party

Now that I need to be more careful about my diet, when I am invited to a get-together, I offer to bring a dish. That way, I ensure that there is always something gluten free for me to eat. Great dishes to take to parties include Vegetable and Olive Platter with White Bean Hummus (page 24); Indian-Style Chickpea Salad (page 48); Quinoa Tabbouleh (page 55); White Bean, Tuna, Fennel, and Olive Salad (page 73); and more.

Cooking with the Seasons

Even though I am now eating gluten free, it has not altered my general cooking philosophy. For years, I have looked to the seasonal fruits, vegetables, and herbs I find at farmers' markets to inform my home-cooked meals and this still remains true. Relying on fresh produce means I need to do little to them to help the ingredients shine, which in turn helps me create quick and easy meals any night of the week.

Although a great reason to eat seasonally is that the produce simply tastes good when it is able to grow and thrive in its natural climate conditions, I find that in-season fruits and vegetables often cost less than foods that are brought in from far-away places, especially when farmers have a generous supply of a particular item. Buying directly from the farmers adds enjoyment to my shopping routine and I appreciate being able to help these local purveyors keep their businesses thriving.

In addition to what's available in the market stalls, I keep the weather in mind when shopping. On a hot day I might opt for a quick, no-cook salad or dinner grilled al fresco; on a cool day, I may crave a comforting braise or warm, oven-roasted meal. Use the chart at right to help inspire your own cooking throughout the year.

Seasonal Produce

The list below provides guidance on the peak seasons for fruits, vegetables, and herbs. Local climates can vary, so the offerings may be different in your area.

Spring

- Asparagus
- Baby kale
- Carrots
- English peas
- Green beans
- Green onions
- Herbs: chives, cilantro, dill, mint, and parsley
- Lettuces
- New potatoes
- Sugar snap peas
- Radishes
- Spinach
- Strawberries
- Wild mushrooms

Summer

- Bell peppers
- Chiles
- Corn
- Cucumbers
- Eggplants
- Green beans
- Greens: arugula and spinach
- Herbs: basil, mint, and parsley
- Melons
- Tomatoes
- Stone fruits
- Summer squashes

Fall

- Apples
- Broccoli
- Brussels sprouts
- Cauliflower
- Hearty greens: kale and chard
- Herbs: bay leaves, rosemary, and sage
- Parsnips
- Pears
- Sweet potatoes
- Wild mushrooms
- Winter squashes

Winter

- Cabbage
- Citrus fruits
- Fennel
- Hearty greens: kale and chard
- Herbs: rosemary and sage
- Parsnips
- Sweet potatoes
- Watercress
- Winter squashes

Building a Gluten-Free Pantry

I have found that having on hand a good supply of pantry staples provides a solid foundation for quickly putting together meals throughout the week. Stocking the pantry requires a little extra thought when you are living a gluten-free lifestyle, but if your cupboard is well curated with such things as gluten-free dried pastas and grains; canned beans and tomatoes; a good supply of condiments and sauces; prepared gluten-free broths; flavorful spices; and tempting snacks, you should only need to shop a couple times a week for perishable ingredients.

The checklist at right features the pantry items that I used to build the recipes in this book. Use it as a personal checklist, or as a template for customizing your own gluten-free pantry. Turn to page 216 for a list of sources for quality gluten-free products that I personally recommend.

If you or a loved one has a gluten intolerance or sensitivity, you'll want to take extra care when buying pantry ingredients. Be sure always to read package labels. Even some things that are naturally gluten-free are sometimes made in facilities that make products that contain gluten and can become contaminated during manufacturing or packaging. Also, product can change, so check labels frequently.

Gluten-Free Pantry Checklist

Below is a list of basic kitchen staples that are used in many of the recipes in this book. Keep a supply of the following items on hand and you'll be able to make tempting gluten-free meals anytime.

Condiments & Sauces

- ☐ Asian fish sauce
- ☐ Balsamic vinegar
- ☐ Dijon mustard
- ☐ Extra-virgin olive oil
- ☐ Gluten-free beef, chicken, and vegetable broth
- ☐ Gluten-free chile paste
- ☐ Gluten-free hoisin sauce
- ☐ Gluten-free ketchup
- ☐ Gluten-free mayonnaise
- ☐ Gluten-free tamari
- ☐ Gluten-free tomato paste
- ☐ Pomegranate molasses
- ☐ Sherry vinegar
- ☐ Thai-style curry paste

Spices

- ☐ Ancho chile powder
- ☐ Cayenne pepper
- ☐ Dried marjoram
- ☐ Fennel seeds
- ☐ Ground chipotle chile
- ☐ Ground coriander
- ☐ Ground cumin
- ☐ Kosher salt
- ☐ Peppercorns
- ☐ Red pepper flakes
- ☐ Smoked paprika
- ☐ Sweet paprika

Staples

- ☐ Bean thread noodles
- ☐ Brown basmati or jasmine rice
- ☐ Canned beans
- ☐ Canned tomatoes
- ☐ Coconut milk
- ☐ Gluten-free chickpea/ garbanzo bean flour
- ☐ Gluten-free corn tortillas
- ☐ Gluten-free cornmeal
- ☐ Gluten-free flour mix
- ☐ Gluten-free oats
- ☐ Gluten-free pasta
- ☐ Gluten-free polenta
- ☐ Quinoa
- ☐ Rice noodles
- ☐ Rice sticks
- ☐ Rice

Snacks

- ☐ Gluten-free crackers
- ☐ Gluten-free multigrain snack chips
- ☐ Gluten-free rice crackers
- ☐ Gluten-free tortilla chips

Cooking Efficiently

For me, dinner planning starts with the raw ingredients: I let what's fresh and in season be the star of my meals. But once I decide on a dish, a handful of smart strategies, such as those that follow, help ensure I can get a delicious gluten-free meal on the table in minutes.

Plan ahead

If I know that I'll be pressed for time during the week, I will plan my meals and shop for my meat, poultry, and fish on the weekend. Once I get home, I'll wrap, label, and freeze what I won't be using within the next couple of days (remember to move the frozen items to the refrigerator to thaw on the night before you will need them). Alternatively, if I know I'm going to be near my farmers' market, butcher, or fishmonger during the week, I'll plan my meals around a stop at my favorite establishments. When shopping at the farmers' market, I like to keep my eye out for vegetables that can be simply prepared—steamed, sautéed, roasted—to accompany gluten-free meals.

Stay organized

I assemble and measure all of my ingredients before I begin cooking. That way, I won't need to search for ingredients at the last minute and the kitchen won't be cluttered. Also, I aim to use as few pans as possible when preparing meals. Not only does this streamline the cooking process, but also it saves time in cleanup.

Be creative

Rethink what's appropriate for dinner. Some of the most popular suppers in my house include items that you might normally think of as breakfast or lunch foods; for example, egg dishes, tacos, wraps, and pizzas are favorites.

Time it right

I keep quick-cooking quinoa and brown basmati or jasmine rice in the cupboard and put them on to cook before prepping the other ingredients for the meal. The grains are ready to serve when the entrée is finished. See pages 74 and 214 for basic recipes.

Top it off

Consider cold sauces, such as naturally gluten-free salsas, pestos, raitas, and vinaigrettes. These versatile mixtures can often be made ahead of time—and in large batches—to be used with tonight's meal as well as others during the week. Turn to pages 214–215 for inspiration, or use your own favorites.

Make more to store

To save time in the kitchen, I like to prepare a double batch of a dish and save the second helping to serve later. You can make such things as a soup or stew, roast chicken, or grilled vegetables on the weekend and use them to make quick meals the following week. I also like to make a big batch of quinoa or rice to make grain salads with cut-up ingredients.

Making the Most of Your Meals

In my house, "leftovers" is not a dirty word. In fact, the meals eaten on ensuing days are often some of my favorites, thanks to their deepened, well-integrated flavors. The best feature of this make-more-to-store philosophy is knowing that dinner is waiting for me when I return home from a busy day.

Aim for extras

Since my schedule is so full, I've started the habit of imagining new meals I can make with the leftovers of tonight's dinner. My household consists of just two people, but I'll often make recipes that serve four with the intention of having leftovers. Tossed with cooked rice, quinoa, or gluten-free pasta, and flavored with a bold vinaigrette or simple sauce, these dishes become welcome treats on subsequent nights.

Cook on the weekend

On my days off, when I tend to spend more leisurely time in the kitchen, I might roast an extra chicken or grill an extra steak or two to turn into salads, wraps, or pasta dishes for an upcoming night.

Fold and serve

Many leftovers make great taco fillings: Cut meat, poultry, fish, or vegetables into bite-sized pieces and heat through in a frying pan. Serve with warmed gluten-free corn tortillas and purchased salsa.

Simmer your supper

I love to turn leftovers into hearty soups: Sauté a chopped onion, add a couple of cans of drained beans and broth, then whatever leftover vegetables, meat, or poultry are in the refrigerator.

Tips for storing leftovers

Following are eight simple tips to ensure your leftovers stay fresh and wholesome and will become delicious meals in their own right.

- Let food cool slightly before refrigerating, then chill before freezing.
- Transfer the cooled food to an airtight plastic or glass container, leaving room for expansion if freezing.
- Store leftovers in the refrigerator for up to 4 days or in the freezer for up to 4 months.
- Freeze food in small batches, which allows you to heat up just enough to serve one or two people.
- Clearly label items for freezing with the dish name and date they were made. Remember to move them to the refrigerator a day before eating so they can be reheated quickly.
- Be sure to thaw frozen foods in the refrigerator or in the microwave (to avoid bacterial contamination); never thaw them at room temperature.
- Don't crowd foods in the refrigerator or freezer. Air should circulate freely to keep foods evenly cooled.
- As you plan your weekly meals, check the contents of the refrigerator to determine what ingredients should be used that week. Aim to eat leftovers within a day or two.

Basic Recipes

Following are a handful of recipes for healthy grains, starchy vegetables, and quick accompaniments that can round out gluten-free meals.

Brown Jasmine or Basmati Rice

Brown basmati or jasmine rice, 1 cup (7 oz/295 g)

In a saucepan, bring 1½ cups (12 fl oz/375 ml) salted water to a boil. Add the rice and return to a boil. Reduce the heat to low, cover, and cook for 30 minutes. Keep the pan covered, turn off the heat, and let stand for 5 minutes. Fluff the rice with a fork and serve.

MAKES 4 SERVINGS

Quick Mashed Potatoes

Russet potatoes, 1½ lb (750 g), peeled
Butter or olive oil, 2 tablespoons
Kosher salt and freshly ground black pepper

Cut the potatoes into ¾-inch (2-cm) pieces and cook in boiling salted water until tender, about 15 minutes. Drain potatoes, reserving about ½ cup (4 fl oz/125 ml) of the cooking liquid, and return to the hot pot. Using a fork, mash the potatoes coarsely, thinning them to the desired consistency with the reserved cooking liquid. Stir in the butter or olive oil and season to taste with salt and pepper. Serve right away.

MAKES 4 SERVINGS

Quick Mashed Sweet Potatoes

Sweet potatoes, 1½ lb (750 g), peeled
Butter or olive oil, 2 tablespoons
Fresh herbs such as thyme, sage, or flat-leaf parsley, about 2 teaspoons minced (optional)
Kosher salt and freshly ground black pepper

Cut the potatoes into ½–¾-inch (12 mm–2 cm) pieces and steam over boiling salted water until tender, about 15 minutes.

Transfer to a bowl, reserving about ½ cup (4 fl oz/ 125 ml) of the steaming liquid. Using a fork, mash the potatoes coarsely, thinning them to the desired consistency with the reserved steaming liquid. Stir in the butter or olive oil and herbs, if using, and season to taste with salt and pepper. Serve right away.

MAKES 4 SERVINGS

Arugula-Lemon Pesto

Shallot, ½ small
Baby arugula, 1 cup (1 oz/30 g) packed
Toasted almonds, ¼ cup (1 oz/30 g)
Extra-virgin olive oil, ¼ cup (2 fl oz/60 ml)
Lemon zest, 1 teaspoon finely grated
Fresh lemon juice, 1 tablespoon
Kosher salt and freshly ground pepper

Place the shallot in a food processor and mince. Add the arugula and almonds and process until finely ground. With the machine running, gradually add the oil and process just until incorporated. Blend in the lemon zest and juice. Season to taste with salt and pepper. Use right away, or cover and refrigerate for up to 3 days. Bring to room temperature before serving.

MAKES 4 SERVINGS

Mint Pesto

Fresh mint leaves, ¼ cup (¼ oz/8 g) packed
Toasted whole almonds, ¼ cup (1 oz/30 g)
Shallot, ½ small
Extra-virgin olive oil, ¼ cup (2 fl oz/60 ml)
Fresh lemon juice, 1½ teaspoons
Kosher salt and freshly ground pepper

In a food processor, combine the mint, almonds, and shallot and process until finely ground. With the machine running, gradually add the oil. Mix in the lemon juice, and then season to taste with salt and pepper. Use right away, or cover and refrigerate for up to 3 days. Bring to room temperature before serving.

MAKES 4 SERVINGS

Salsa Verde

Extra-virgin olive oil, ½ cup (4 fl oz/125 ml)
Fresh flat-leaf parsley, ⅓ cup (½ oz/15 g) minced
Green onions, 3, thinly sliced
Lemon zest, 1½ teaspoons grated
Fresh lemon juice, 1½ tablespoons
Kosher salt and freshly ground pepper

In a small bowl, combine the oil, parsley, green onions, lemon zest, and juice. Season to taste with salt and pepper. Use right away, or cover and refrigerate for up to 3 days. Bring to room temperature before serving.

MAKES 4 SERVINGS

Quick Guacamole

Fresh cilantro, ¼ cup (⅓ oz/10 g) minced
Fresh lime juice, 2 tablespoons
Asian chile paste such as sambal oelek or Sriracha, 1 teaspoon
Kosher salt, ¼ teaspoon
Ripe avocados, 2, peeled and cut into ½–¾-inch (12 mm–2 cm) pieces

In a medium bowl, combine the cilantro, lime juice, chile paste, and salt and crush together with a fork. Add the avocados and mix in, crushing slightly. Transfer to a serving bowl and serve right away.

MAKES 4 SERVINGS

Asian Slaw

Vegetable oil, 3 tablespoons
Rice vinegar, 2 tablespoons
Fresh ginger, ½ tablespoons minced
Sugar, 1½ teaspoons
Asian sesame oil, 1½ teaspoons
Asian chile paste such as sambal oelek, ¾ teaspoon
Napa cabbage, 6 cups (18 oz/560 g) thinly sliced (about ½ large head)
Green onions, 4, thinly sliced
Kosher salt and freshly ground pepper
Toasted sesame seeds, 1 tablespoon (optional)

In a small bowl, combine the vegetable oil, vinegar, ginger, sugar, sesame oil, and chile paste to make a dressing. In a large bowl, combine the cabbage and sliced green onions. Add the dressing and toss to coat. Season to taste with salt and pepper. Sprinkle with sesame seeds, if using. Let stand for a few minutes to blend the flavors.

MAKES 4 SERVINGS

Sweetened Whipped Cream

Cold heavy cream, ½ cup (4 fl oz/125 ml)
Sugar, 2 teaspoons
Pure vanilla extract, ½ teaspoon

In a chilled bowl, combine the heavy cream, sugar, and vanilla. Using an electric mixer beat on medium-high speed until soft peaks form. Use the cream right away, or cover and refrigerate until serving time.

MAKES ABOUT 1 CUP (8 FL OZ/250 ML)

Gluten-Free Sources

Following are some of my favorite products for gluten-free eating. If you are suffering from a gluten intolerance or sensitivity, it is important to read labels carefully and, when in doubt, to check directly with manufacturers. Commercial brands change their formulations frequently, so check often.

All-Purpose Flour Mix

Bob's Red Mill Gluten-Free All-Purpose Baking Flour
www.bobsredmill.com/gluten-free

Cup4Cup Gluten-Free Flour
www.cup4cup.com
www.williams-sonoma.com/products/
cup4cup-gluten-free-flour/

King Arthur Gluten-free Multi-Purpose Flour
www.kingarthurflour.com/glutenfree

Bread and Buns

Mariposa Bakery
www.mariposabaking.com

Udi's
udisglutenfree.com

Broths

Swanson Natural Goodness in asceptic packages: chicken broth, chicken stock, beef stock; and in cans: chicken broth, vegetable broth
www.swansonbroth.com

Chickpea (Garbanzo Bean) Flour

Bob's Red Mill Gluten-Free Garbanzo Bean Flour
www.bobsredmill.com/gluten-free

Chile Paste

Huy Fong
Sriracha and Sambal Oelek
www.huyfong.com

Chips

Food Should Taste Good
multigrain, sweet potato, blue corn and other tortilla chips
www.foodshouldtastegood.com

Garden of Eatin' Sesame Blues and other tortilla chips
www.gardenofeatin.com

Late July Organic Snacks Multigrain Snack Chips
www.latejuly.com

Corn Flakes

Nature's Path Fruit Juice Sweetened Corn Flakes
www.us.naturespath.com

Erewhon Organic Cornflakes
www.attunefoods.com/products/
Erewhon-Gluten-Free

Cornmeal

Bob's Red Mill Gluten-Free Cornmeal
www.bobsredmill.com/gluten-free

Crackers
Blue Diamond Nut Thins
www.bluediamond.com

Hoisin Sauce
Dynasty Hoisin Sauce
www.jfc.com

Ketchup
Heinz Ketchup
www.heinz.com/glutenfree/products.html

Oats
Bob's Red Mill Gluten-Free Oats
www.bobsredmill.com/gluten-free

Gluten-Free Oats.com
www.glutenfreeoats.com

Trader Joe's Gluten-Free Rolled Oats
www.traderjoes.com/lists/no-gluten.asp

Mayonnaise
Best Foods Real Mayonnaise
www.bestfoods.com

Hellmann's Real Mayonnaise
www.hellmanns.com

Pasta
Ancient Harvest Quinoa Pasta
(made with corn flour and quinoa flour)
www.quinoa.net/145/163.html

Schar Gluten-Free Grain Pasta
(made with corn flour, rice flour, and pea protein)
www.schar.elsstore.com/

Rice Noodles
Annie Chun's Pad Thai Noodles
www.anniechun.com

Dynasty
beanthread noodles (Saifun), rice sticks (Maifun)
www.jfc.com

Tamari
San J Organic Gluten-Free Tamari
www.san-J.com

Tortillas
La Tortilla Factory's Smart and Delicious Fiber
and Flax Corn Tortillas
www.latortillafactory.com

Index

weldon**owen**

415 Jackson Street, Suite 200, San Francisco, CA 94111
www.weldonowen.com

Weldon Owen is a division of
BONNIER

WELDON OWEN, INC.	**WEEKNIGHT GLUTEN FREE**
CEO and President Terry Newell	Conceived and produced by Weldon Owen, Inc.
VP, Sales and Marketing Amy Kaneko	In collaboration with Williams-Sonoma, Inc.
Director of Finance Mark Perrigo	3250 Van Ness Avenue, San Francisco, CA 94109
VP and Publisher Hannah Rahill	**A WELDON OWEN PRODUCTION**
Executive Editor Jennifer Newens	Copyright © 2013 Weldon Owen, Inc. and Williams-Sonoma, Inc.
	All rights reserved, including the right of reproduction
Creative Director Emma Boys	in whole or in part in any form.
Senior Art Director Kara Church	
Designer Rachel Lopez Metzger	Printed and bound by Toppan-Leefung in China
Production Director Chris Hemesath	First printed in 2013
Production Manager Michelle Duggan	10 9 8 7 6 5 4 3 2
Photographer Kate Sears	Library of Congress Control Number: 2012952969
Food Stylist Lillian Kang	
Prop Stylist Christine Wolheim	ISBN13: 978-1-61628-500-5
	ISBN 10: 1-61628-500-1

ACKNOWLEDGMENTS
Weldon Owen wishes to thank the following people for their generous support in producing this book:
Amanda Anselmino, Anna Grace, Eve Lynch, Elizabeth Parson, Virginia Rainey, and Victoria Harris

PHOTO CREDITS
All photos by Kate Sears except: Steve Peck, page 6, left;
Ray Kachatorian, page 6 middle and right; page 7, and page 153.
Tucker + Hossler, page 105.